How to Pass

SECOND EDITION

NATIONAL 5

Computing Science

David Alford

HODDER
GIBSON
AN HACHETTE UK COMPANY

The Publishers would like to thank the following for permission to reproduce copyright material.

Photo credits

p.1 © Dawn Gilfillan/Shutterstock; **p.4** © nd3000/Shutterstock; **p.10** Scratch is developed by the Lifelong Kindergarten Group at the MIT Media Lab. See http://scratch.mit.edu; **p.28** l, r © Used with permission from Microsoft; **p.72** © Vintage Tone/Shutterstock; **p.83** © photon_photo/stock.adobe.com; **p.86** © Atlaspix/Shutterstock; **p.83** © photon_photo/stock.adobe.com; **p.89** © Titima Ongkantong/Shutterstock; **p.96** t © Sashkin/Shutterstock; **p.96** b © Nor Gal/Shutterstock; **p.97** © Iaroslav Neliubov/Shutterstock; **p.100** © sdecoret/Shutterstock; **p.101** © Elnur/stock.adobe.com; **p.102** © Blend Images/Alamy; **p.103** © Joe Techapanupreeda/Shutterstock; **p.106** © Crown Copyright; **p.108** © Used with permission from Microsoft; **p.111** © Wright Studio./Shutterstock; **p.114** © arka38/Shutterstock; **p.117** © Rawpixel.com/Shutterstock; **p.119** © 2010 Future Publishing/Getty Images; **p.124** © lubashka/stock.adobe.com; **p.125** © REDPIXEL.PL/Shutterstock; **p.136** © ShendArt./Shutterstock.

t = top, b = bottom, c = centre, l = left, r = right

Every effort has been made to trace all copyright holders, but if any have been inadvertently overlooked, the Publishers will be pleased to make the necessary arrangements at the first opportunity.

Although every effort has been made to ensure that website addresses are correct at time of going to press, Hodder Gibson cannot be held responsible for the content of any website mentioned in this book. It is sometimes possible to find a relocated web page by typing in the address of the home page for a website in the URL window of your browser.

Hachette UK's policy is to use papers that are natural, renewable and recyclable products and made from wood grown in sustainable forests. The logging and manufacturing processes are expected to conform to the environmental regulations of the country of origin.

Orders: please contact Bookpoint Ltd, 130 Park Drive, Milton Park, Abingdon, Oxon OX14 4SE. Telephone: (44) 01235 827720. Fax: (44) 01235 400401. Email education@bookpoint.co.uk. Lines are open from 9 a.m. to 5 p.m., Monday to Saturday, with a 24-hour message answering service. Visit our website at www.hoddereducation.co.uk. Hodder Gibson can also be contacted direct at hoddergibson@hodder.co.uk

© David Alford 2018, © Frank Frame 2013

First published in 2018 by

Hodder Gibson, an imprint of Hodder Education

An Hachette UK Company

211 St Vincent Street

Glasgow, G2 5QY

Impression number	5	4	3	2	1
Year	2022	2021	2020	2019	2018

Cover photo © Hellen Sergeyeva/stock.adobe.com

Illustrations by Aptara, Inc.

Typeset in Cronos Pro by Aptara, Inc.
Printed in Spain
A catalogue record for this title is available from the British Library.
ISBN: 978 1 5104 2088 5

Contents

Introduction

The National 5 Computing Science course has been designed to build upon and extend the skills, knowledge and understanding gained in National 4 Computing Science. Of course, some candidates will embark on this course having previously followed the broad general education.

While the course includes many facts about aspects of computing science, the focus is on applying knowledge and understanding within the context of a problem. The aim of the course is to give the candidate both ability and confidence to tackle a range of problems in both familiar and unfamiliar situations.

Course structure

The course consists of four areas of study.

Software design and development

This unit covers the basics of the development process for computer programs. You will learn how to analyse a problem, design a solution, implement that design as a program, test your program and evaluate the success of your program. You will develop your problem-solving skills and you will also learn to interpret existing designs and programs.

Computer systems

You will gain knowledge of the inside of the computer, including the basic layout and workings of the processor and memory, called computer architecture. You will learn how computers can affect the environment and you will learn about how to counter some of the threats to a computer system.

Database design and development

This unit covers the basics of the development process of databases. You will learn how to analyse the requirements of a database problem, design a solution, implement that design as a database, test your database queries and evaluate the success of your database solution. You will learn how to develop a database and how to implement SQL to interact with the data contained within your database. You will also learn the implications of the Data Protection Act 1998 for database development.

Web design and development

This unit covers the basics of the development process of websites. You will learn how to analyse the requirements of a web-based problem, design a solution, implement that design as a website, test that your website functions as expected and evaluate the success of your web-based solution. You will learn how to implement both HTML and CSS to produce web pages, and you will learn the implications of the Copyright Designs and Patents Act 1988 for web development.

Course assessment

The course assessment involves a total of 160 marks; 110 marks are assessed through the question paper and 50 marks are assessed through the assignment.

The question paper

The question paper in the May examination period is worth 110 marks. It will be a two-hour closed-book examination with printed questions to which you will have to write your answers. Questions will be set within a context so that you must exhibit your skills in problem-solving as well as the knowledge and understanding that you have gained throughout the course.

The question paper has two sections. Section 1 consists of 25 marks of short-answer questions; Section 2 consists of 85 marks of context-based questions which will be longer with many parts.

Across the paper, the four areas of study will have a different number of marks allocated to them.
- Software design and development: 34–44 marks, approximately 40% of the marks in the paper.
- Computer systems: 12–20 marks, approximately 10% of the marks in the paper.
- Database design and development: 20–35 marks, approximately 25% of the marks in the paper.
- Web design and development: 20–35 marks, approximately 25% of the marks in the paper.

You will also see the different stages of the development process will have a different number of marks allocated to them.
- Analysis: 0–6 marks, approximately 5% of the marks in the paper.
- Design: 35–51 marks, approximately 30% of the marks in the paper.
- Implementation: 26–42 marks, approximately 40% of the marks in the paper.
- Testing: 7–15 marks, approximately 10% of the marks in the paper.
- Evaluation: 0–6 marks, approximately 5% of the marks in the paper.
- Computer systems: 12–20 marks, approximately 10% of the marks in the paper.

The assignment

The assignment will have 50 marks available. It will feature a task on database design and development, a task on software design and development, and a task on web design and development.

The assignment is an open-book assessment.

There is a new assignment released each year, valid only for that year. You are allowed a total of eight hours to complete the assignment. The assignment is sent away to the SQA to be marked. It will not be reviewed by your teacher and returned to you for improvement. There is no word limit or page limit.

The tasks will have marks assigned as follows.
- Software design and development: 25 marks, 50% of the marks in the assignment.
- Database design and development: 10–15 marks, approximately 25% of the marks in the assignment.
- Web design and development: 10–15 marks, approximately 25% of the marks in the assignment.

You will also see the different stages of the development process will have a different number of marks allocated to them.
- Analysis: 5 marks, 10% of the marks in the assignment.
- Design: 5 marks, 10% of the marks in the assignment.
- Implementation: 30 marks, 60% of the marks in the assignment.
- Testing: 5 marks, 10% of the marks in the assignment.
- Evaluation: 5 marks, 10% of the marks in the assignment.

Hints & tips

✓ Draw up a revision plan well ahead of the exam. Make sure you create a schedule that lets you cover all of the topics, without leaving everything to the last minute.

✓ Use a checklist to make sure you cover all of the course content.

✓ Make sure you know all the important definitions in this book (the Glossary will help you to with this).

✓ Check that your knowledge is up to exam standards by answering all of the questions in this book (suggested answers are at the back).

✓ Look on the SQA website for the specimen assignment, specimen examination paper, past papers and marking instructions.

✓ Consider buying Practice Papers for National 5 Computing Science published by Hodder Gibson, details can be found at www.hoddereducation.co.uk.

Section 1 Software Design and Development

Analysis and design (software)

What you should know

By the end of this chapter you should **know** and **understand**:

★ that the development methodology used in National 5 is an iterative development process with six stages – analysis, design, implementation, testing, documentation and evaluation
★ that in the analysis stage you must identify the purpose and functional requirements of a problem, in terms of inputs, processes and outputs
★ the five data types in use at National 5 level – character, string, numeric (integer and real) and Boolean
★ the two data structures in use at National 5 level – variable and one-dimensional array
★ how to create or interpret the three design notations in use at National 5 level – structure diagrams, flowcharts and pseudocode
★ how to design a user interface using a wireframe, showing input and output.

The software development process

The approach that programmers take to solving a problem is known as the **development methodology**.

At National 5 level, the development methodology used is a development process with six stages:

1 analysis
2 design
3 implementation
4 testing
5 documentation
6 evaluation.

This process is an **iterative** process, because it is repetitive. This means that earlier stages in the process often have to be revisited as a result of information gained at later stages in the process.

Below is one scenario in which we see the iterative nature of the software development process.

Example

Sandeep has written a program to count how many pupils in an S4 class are old enough to leave school should they wish. You have to be 16 years old to leave school. At the **testing stage**, one test run uses the following data as input to the program:

Name	Age
Wiktor	15
Alan	15
Karen	16
Lucy	16
Dean	16

The output from the program is this:

```
The number of pupils old enough to leave school
is 2
```

Sandeep notices that this output is incorrect. There is a **logic error** in the program. Sandeep must return to the **design stage** in order to correct the error, and then revisit the **implementation stage**, before returning to the testing stage once more.

The analysis stage

The **analysis stage** is where the programmers look at the problem and decide exactly what must be included within the program in order to solve the problem.

If you are given a problem you will have to be able to produce an analysis as a document which includes:

- the purpose of the program
- what features the program must have in order to fully solve the problem (these are the **functional requirements**)
- the range and type of data to be entered into the program (inputs) with any relevant **input validation** to be included
- what the program will do with the data entered (processes)
- what the program must produce as it runs (outputs).

Input validation

Validation is including code in your program so that data entered is repeatedly checked to ensure that it is sensible. If data entered as an input is not within the acceptable limits, the user should be shown a useful message to help them understand why the input wasn't accepted. The program should then allow the user to re-enter the data. However, the program should continue to check the data that has been input until the entry is acceptable, that is, until the data is **valid**.

Below is an example problem with corresponding analysis to help you.

Example

The distance to walk from Glasgow to Edinburgh is 71 133 metres. However, it has been estimated that the average person walks 798 metres in a normal day. At that rate it would take over 89 days to walk from Glasgow to Edinburgh. The pupils at Muirshiel Primary school have decided that they will all wear devices to measure how many metres that they walk in one month. On the last day of the month they will type in to a program the number of metres that they have walked (for example 72 434.75), and the program should tell them whether or not they have successfully walked the distance between Glasgow and Edinburgh. The number of metres entered must be more than or equal to zero. You are to write this program.

Analysis

I have to write a program that will tell users whether they have walked the distance in metres between Glasgow and Edinburgh.

The program must accept and validate a positive number of metres, check if the number of metres is greater than or equal to 71 133 and show a relevant message on the screen.

Inputs: distance – a real number variable that must be validated to be zero or more.

Process: check if the distance is more than or equal to 71 133.

Outputs: a message indicating if the pupil walked enough miles to travel between Glasgow and Edinburgh or not.

The completed statement like the one above of exactly what the problem involves is often called the **software specification**. It is a clear statement of the problem to be solved.

Assumptions

In some cases it may also be necessary to state assumptions as part of your analysis. This is where the problem given is unclear on one or more specific parts of the program to be created. You would then make your own sensible decision and include it in the assumptions section of the analysis. A possible assumption for the above program might be: 'the program will be run once for each pupil, so it is not necessary to ask for the total number of pupils and include a loop'.

Questions ?

1. Complete a full analysis for this problem.
   Speed bumps and other traffic-calming measures can protect children who are playing, but can feel like a nuisance to drivers. A program is required that can be used at a community meeting to help a housing estate decide whether they want speed bumps installed or not. When the program is run, the user should be asked how many homes are in the estate and then the program should ask each homeowner to enter 'yes' or 'no' to whether they want speed bumps or not. The program should then tell the residents how many voted 'yes', and whether or not speed bumps will be brought in. The estate will have new speed bumps installed if more than half of the residents voted for them.

2. What is a development methodology?
3. **a)** What is an iterative process?
   b) How could the software development process be said to be an iterative process?
4. What is the software specification?

The design stage

In the **design stage**, the programming team will plan how they are going to solve the problem given.

In the design phase the problem is broken down into 'chunks' and each chunk is then broken down further and further until the little bits are easy to solve in any programming language. The solution to the problem is called the '**algorithm**', a fancy word for a plan.

Often at this stage, it is decided what **data types** and **data structures** will be used for each item of data used within the program.

Data structures

A **variable** can be used to hold one item of data. Often when a variable is declared it is given a name and a data type.

An array can be used to hold a number of related items of data. In National 5, you will only encounter **one-dimensional arrays**. When a one-dimensional array is declared, it is given a name, a data type and a size (the number of items, or elements, it can hold). This means that each element in the array must be of the same data type.

Data types

In National 5, there are five data types that you must be able to use.

Data type	Description	Examples
Character	Any one punctuation symbol, letter or number that can be typed from the keyboard	A, z, &
String	A sequence of characters	Hello there, John, 08001111
Integer	A numeric data type, for whole numbers	35, 2017, 0
Real	A numeric data type, for numbers with a fractional part	0.2, 1.5, 3.14159265359
Boolean	True or false only	true, false

Design notations

The programmer(s) will write a detailed plan of steps to be taken to solve the problem. The way that they choose to write this plan down is called the **design notation**. There are three design notations that you must be able to read and understand: **structure diagrams**, **flowcharts** and **pseudocode**.

Key point !

Structure diagram

A structure diagram begins with the problem in a box at the top. It is broken down into sub-problems which are contained within one of four possible symbols according to the key shown below. It is possible for a sub-problem to be further broken down as appropriate, until it can be solved in one line of code. In a structure diagram, sub-problems are shown from left to right according to the order they would be completed in, first at the left, last at the right.

Structure diagram key	
▭	A process: any action or collection of actions that doesn't fit into the three categories below this.
▢ or ⬭	A loop: actions listed below this will be repeated. The symbol should contain the number of times to be repeated (if showing a **fixed loop**) or the conditions for the repeating to continue or end (if showing a **conditional loop**).
⬡	Selection: this should contain a question about some data from the program. Branches coming down from this should be labelled to show which branch is taken for each possible answer to the question.
▯▯	A pre-defined process: this should be used if the **function** to be used is already part of the programming language, for example, rounding a number.

Example

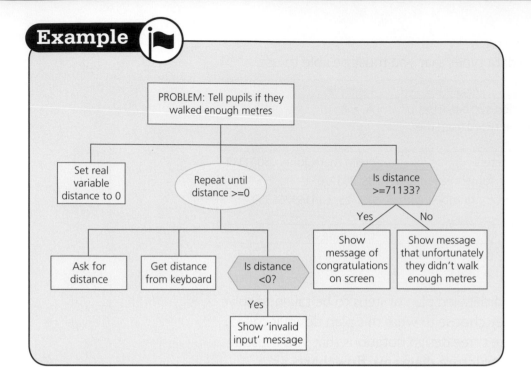

PROBLEM: Tell pupils if they walked enough metres

Set real variable distance to 0

Repeat until distance >=0

Is distance >=71133?

Yes / No

Ask for distance

Get distance from keyboard

Is distance <0?

Show message of congratulations on screen

Show message that unfortunately they didn't walk enough metres

Yes

Show 'invalid input' message

Key point (!)

Flowchart

The flowchart shows the order of execution of instructions from the start at the top, to the end at the bottom. Like the structure diagram, different symbols are used for different types of instructions. However, there is no symbol for a loop, instead the arrows combined with a decision are used.

Flowchart key

▭	A process: any action or collection of actions that doesn't fit into the categories below this.
◖▭◗	Terminal: used for the start and end of the problem.
⬡	Initialisation: used when a variable or array is being declared or being assigned an initial value.
▱	Input/output: used when data is brought in to the program (for example, from the keyboard) or data is sent out from the program (for example, show a message on screen).
◇	Decision: this should contain a question about some data from the program. Branches coming down from this should be labelled to show which branch is taken for each possible answer to the question.
▐▌	A pre-defined process: this should be used if the function to be used is already part of the programming language, for example, rounding a number.
○	On-page connector: used to show that a flowchart should continue onto a new page, but instead keeps it on the same page.

Example

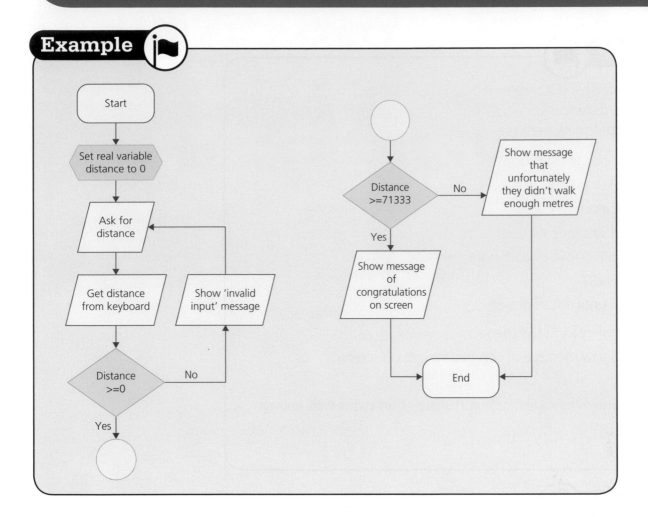

Key points

Pseudocode

Pseudocode is a text-based method of designing a program that uses a language that is halfway between ordinary language and programming code.

You will use pseudocode to break down the problem you are given into ever smaller steps until you can code it.

The steps used are similar to those in the structure diagram.

Example

1 Set real variable distance to 0.
2 Get valid distance.
3 Show appropriate message.

    2.1 Start conditional loop

        2.2 Ask for distance

        2.3 Get distance

        2.4 If distance <0 then

            2.5 Show 'invalid input' message

        2.6 End if

    2.7 Loop until distance >=0

    3.1 If distance>=71133 then

        3.2 Show message of congratulations on screen

    3.3 Else

        3.4 Show message that unfortunately they didn't walk enough metres

    3.5 End if

Questions

5 What three pieces of information are used when declaring an array within a program?
6 What kind of data might be stored in:
   a) a real variable?
   b) a Boolean variable?
7 What is a design notation?

Activity

1 Using the situation from Question 1 on p.4, plan the solution using each of the three design notations.

Wireframe

In National 5, you will design the user interface for programs and web pages using a **wireframe**. A wireframe is a labelled plan of what will be on the screen.

Here is a checklist of what to include in a wireframe for a program:
- areas where the user will input data
- areas that may change to show output of data
- areas that link to another page/file/screen
- any sound that will be heard
- any image file that will be included
- font information (size, font name, formatting, colour)
- all colour information.

Example

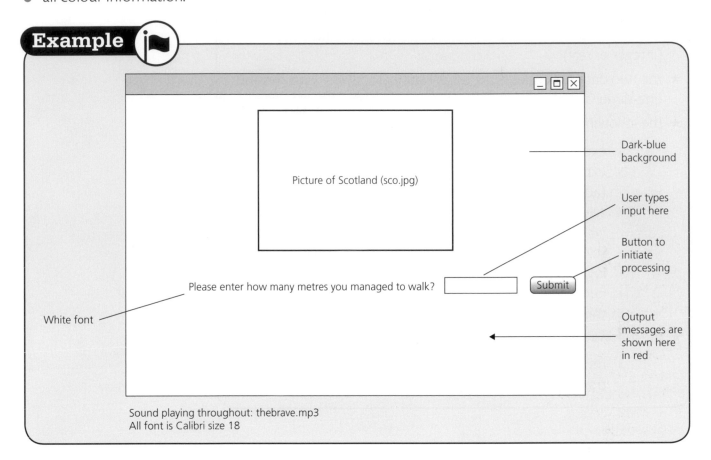

2 Sea Salvage is a new game app for smartphone and tablet where the user controls a diver swimming through underwater tunnels. Divers must avoid sharp rocks and collect treasure. Design a wireframe for this game app.

Implementation (Scratch)

What you should know

By the end of this chapter you should **know** and **understand** how to use the Scratch development environment to implement:

★ the two data types available in Scratch – string and numeric (integer or real)

★ the two data structures required at National 5 level – variables and one-dimensional arrays

★ the following **constructs**:

   ★ expressions to assign values
   ★ expressions to return values using arithmetic operations (addition, subtraction, multiplication, division)
   ★ selection constructs using simple conditional statements with <, >, = operators
   ★ selection constructs using complex conditional statements
   ★ logical operators (AND, OR, NOT)
   ★ iteration and repetition using fixed and conditional loops
   ★ the 'random' predefined function

★ the following standard algorithms:

   ★ running total within loop
   ★ traversing a one-dimensional array.

Getting numbers into your program

In this section you are going to learn how to get whole numbers into your program.

Making a variable to store whole numbers

Using the *variables* window you can make and name a variable as shown in the screenshot. You can even set, change, show and hide variables.

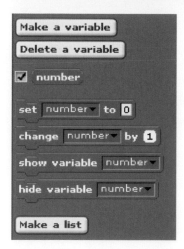

Make a variable and call it *Number* as shown in the screenshot above. Open the *sensing* window and use the *ask* and *answer* blocks to enter a number.

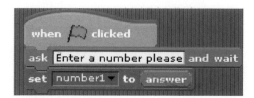

The number you enter will appear on the screen as shown in the screenshot below:

Save your program as Example1.

Activities

1 Write a program that asks for and displays the number of people in your family. Save it as Scratch Activity 1.
2 Write a program that asks for and displays the number of hours you watch television each day. Save it as Scratch Activity 2.
3 Create a program that:
   ● enters the cost of a mobile phone
   ● enters the cost of a games app for a phone.

Assigning variables

This means you can set the value of a number. In Scratch you do this by using the *set* block.

This block assigns a number to the variable *cost of 1 phone call* as shown in the screenshot below.

This block assigns a number to the variable *cost of 1 text message* as shown in the screenshot below:

Enter the program from the screenshot below:

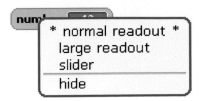

Activity

4 Write a program to assign and display:
- the number of pupils in your class today
- the number of boys in your class
- the number of girls in your class.

Save it as Scratch Activity 4.

Output showing numeric variables

There are four ways to display a variable using Scratch.

The first three are available on the *popup* menu linked to each variable as shown in the screenshot below.

```
num
   * normal readout *
   large readout
   slider
   hide
```

- Normal
- Large
- Slider

The fourth is produced by using a block from the *Looks* window which causes the sprite to output the variable as shown in the screenshot below.

Activity

5 Write a program to assign and display:
- the number of hours you spend doing homework each day
- the number of hours you spend on the internet each day
- the number of hours you spend sleeping each night.

You must display each one in a different way. Save it as Scratch Activity 5.

Getting words into your program

Variables can hold words. They are called string variables. In Scratch you make a string variable in exactly the same way as you make a variable to hold a number. Make a variable called *Name*.

Enter the program from the screenshot below:

Your screen should look something like the screenshot below when you run it:

You can also use the sprite to display your string. Add this block your program:

Fred

Name Fred

Getting words and numbers into your program

This is easy in Scratch! You simply make the variables you want and then set them to the name or number or use the *ask/answer* to enter them.

Enter the program from the screenshot below:

Your screen should look like the screenshot below:

Enter the name of a CD

Bagpipe Music

Adding up numbers

Adding up numbers in Scratch is easy. You simply make the variables you need then use blocks in the *Operators* window as to the right.

You are going to use the operator with the + sign as shown in the screenshot to the right.

Make the variables from the screenshot below:

Enter the program from the screenshot below:

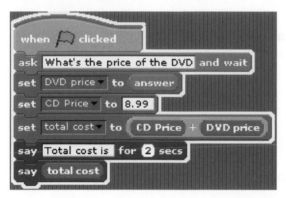

Your screen should look like the screenshot below:

Activities

10 Write a program to add up the cost of two computer games and display the total.
   ● Draw a structure diagram for this program.
   ● Then write the program.
   Save it as Scratch Activity 10.

11 Write a program to add up the cost of two films on DVD and display the average.
   ● Draw a structure diagram for this program.
   ● Then write the program.
   Save it as Scratch Activity 11.   ⇨

⇒
12 Write a program to:
   a) enter the names and cost in pence of each of the following
      grocery items:
      Honey   230
      Salmon   198
      Nuts   125
      Tea   240
      Eggs   175
   b) display the cost of each item and the total cost of all of the items.

The output from your program should look something like the screenshot below:

Egg cost 175
Honey cost 230
Salmon cost 198   total cost 968   968
Nuts cost 125
tea cost 240

You need to complete a report for Activity 12. The report should contain:
● a description of the task
● your structure diagram
● your test data.

You should ask your teacher to check:
● your report
● your coding
● your test run.

Using loops

Fixed loops

In programming we use loops to repeat actions over and over again. A fixed loop is used when the programmer knows how many times the instructions are to be repeated.

Make a variable called *Name of pupil*.

Enter the program from the screenshot below:

Your program should then ask you for the name of a pupil in your class five times.

Your screen should look something like the screenshot below:

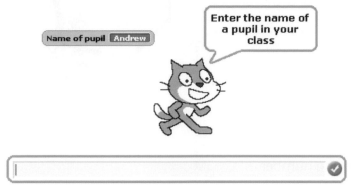

Now enter the program from the screenshot below on the left, which moves the sprite around in a circle by moving 6 × 60 degrees. The screenshot below on the right shows how your screen should look.

 Activity

13 Write a program that:
- asks how many steps a sprite should take
- asks how many degrees it should turn
- moves a sprite around by repeating the moves and turns ten times.
Save it as Scratch Activity 13.

You can use the repeat loop to draw patterns on the screen.

This program uses a repeat loop and blocks from the *pen* window to draw a hexagon.

A hexagon has six sides and the angle of each of the turns is 60 degrees.

Enter the program from the screenshot below:

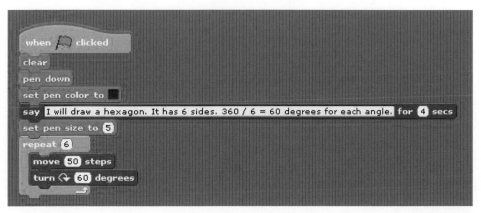

You might have to shrink the sprite down a bit so that it doesn't get in the way of the drawing! Your pattern should look like the screenshot on the right:

14 Write a program that:
- asks the user to enter the number of sides in a drawing
- asks the user to enter the number of steps
- asks the user to enter the degrees of turn
- asks the user to enter the size of the pen
- asks the user to enter the colour of the pen as a number
- draws a pattern.

Test your program using this data

number of sides	8
number of steps	30
degrees of turn	45
size of pen	6
colour of pen	30

Your pattern should look like the screenshot below:

You need to complete a report for Activity 14. The report should contain:
- a description of the task
- your structure diagram
- your test data.

You should ask your teacher to check:
- your report
- your coding
- your test run.

Arithmetical and comparator operators

You have already seen the arithmetic operators below. These are used for:

adding	+
subtraction	–
multiplying	*
division	/

The other operators you need to know about are the ones we use to make comparisons and these are shown in the screenshot below:

less than	<
equals	=
more than	>

Conditional statement

Programmers use a conditional statement (*If*) to get the program to make a decision. For example, your program can decide if a number is too big.

Make a variable called *Number of texts* then enter the program from the screenshot below:

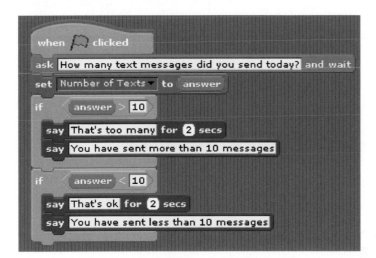

Your screen will look similar to the screenshot below:

Activities

15 Write a program that:
- asks how many pieces of fruit and vegetables you have eaten in the last week
- if it is more than 34 then display a message saying 'Well done, you have eaten five a day!'
- if it is less than 35 then display a message saying 'You should try to eat more fruit and vegetables'.

Save it as Scratch Activity 15.

16 Use an *If* and a simple condition to complete the code in the screenshot on page 12. The *If* should make sure that the size of the pen is no greater than 20!

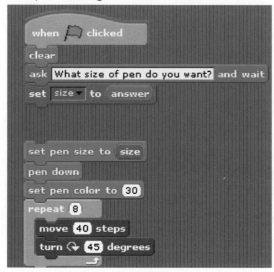

Your screen should look something like the screenshot below:

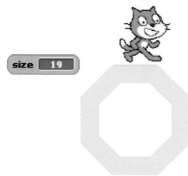

You can use an *If* to give the user a choice as shown in the screenshot below:

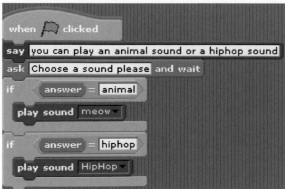

Enter the program shown above.
(You will need headphones to listen to the sound!)

17 Write a program that:
- offers the user a choice of sounds to play
- inputs the reader's choice
- then plays their choice
- and displays a suitable message.

Save it as Scratch Activity 17.

Conditional loops

Loops with simple conditions

Programmers use conditional loops to repeat instructions until or while a certain logical test is true.

In Scratch you use the *Repeat . . . until loop*.

The program in the screenshot below keeps asking for the cost of music downloads in pence until the total is greater than 800.

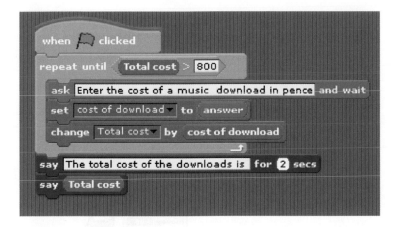

Enter the program above and test it out!

Your screen should look something like the screenshot below:

Activities

18 Write a program to:
- repeatedly ask for the price of sandwiches in pence
- add up the total cost until the total cost is greater than 750 pence
- display a message with the total cost.

Save it as Scratch Activity 18.

19 Write a program to check a password. It should:
- repeat the request for the password until it is correct
- display a message giving authorisation to enter.

Save it as Scratch Activity 19.

You can use repeat loops and conditions to make patterns.

Enter the program from the screenshot below:

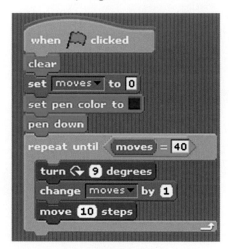

- It clears the screen
- then sets steps to 0
- sets the pen colour to red
- puts the pen down
- repeats until the number of moves = 40
- turns 9 degrees
- adds 1 to the number of moves
- moves 10 steps.

Your screen should look something like the screenshot on the right:

20 Write a program to draw a square. It will have:
- four sides, each side should be around 100 steps
- four 90-degree turns.

Your program should look like the screenshot below:

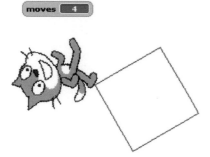

21 Write a program to draw a pattern containing squares, octagons and a circle.
- Your program should use a variety of colours, sizes, sprites and movements to create an interesting colourful display.
- Your program should also ask the user to choose from a range of sounds available to play while the program is running.

You need to complete a report for Activity 21. The report should contain:
- a description of the task
- your structure diagram
- your test data.

You should ask your teacher to check:
- your report
- your coding
- your test run.

Boolean variables

Boolean variables can be set to two values: True or False. They come in useful when, for example, we test the result of a condition.

In Visual Basic this is easy:

```
Dim target_reached as boolean = false ' target_reached is set to false
If total = > 200 Then
    target_reached = true ' target_reached is set to true when the
    condition is met
End If
```

You can then use the Boolean variable as a control for another process:

```
If target_reached = true Then
     call Bonus_display
End If
```

In Scratch there is no Boolean variable and you have to use a workaround as shown in the screenshot below.

You could then use *target_reached* as a Boolean by using target_reached set to 1 as True and target_reached set to 0 as false.

This is a workaround and it is rather awkward, though it does work!

Activity

22 Write a program that uses a Boolean (workaround) variable:
- to check that the answer to each one of three quiz questions is correct
- to add five points to the total score for a correct answer.

Using arrays

An array is a list of numbers or words. Each array has a name. This array is called *Name*.

Index	1	2	3	4
Name	Fred	Ted	Ed	Ned

Each array has an index. The index is used to count down (or up) the array.

So *Name(1)* is Fred, *Name(2)* is Ted and so on.

This array is called Prices.

Index	1	2	3	4
Prices	34.99	12.50	14.30	56.00

Here *Prices(1)* is 34.99, *Prices(2)* is 12.50 and so on.

Setting up and filling an array

The first thing you have to do is set up your array using the *Make a list* block in the *variables* menu as in the screenshot on the right.

Call the list *Grocery Items*. It should appear on your screen. You might have to stretch it to make it bigger! You will need to set up a counter to count down the index as shown in the screenshot below:

 **Activities**

23 **a)** Set up a list called *Grocery Items* and a variable called *counter*, then enter the program in the screenshot below. It:

- sets the counter to 1
- asks for the grocery item
- adds it to the array
- adds 1 to the counter.

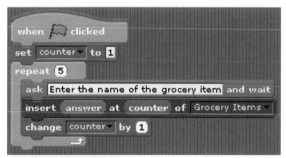

Your screen should look something like the screenshot below:

If you want to you can get a sprite to output the groceries!
Note: Scratch arrays can hold either *strings* or *numbers*.

b) Set up and fill an array to hold the prices of the grocery items. Your screen should look like the screenshot below:

⇨ Now add the scripts from the screenshot below to calculate the average cost:

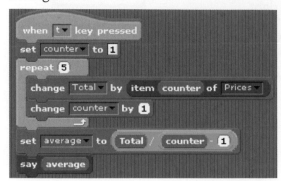

24 Write a program:
- to store the names and chart position of ten songs
- to ask the user to choose a position on the list
- to use the sprite to output the song at that position.

25 Write a program:
- to store the names and costs of five movie DVDs
- to ask for the name of a movie DVD on the list and use a sprite to display the name and price
- to have the sprite say if the movie requested by the user is not on the list!

Drawing patterns

Scratch can be used to draw complex patterns and play sounds. A useful feature is the *random* function shown in the screenshot to the right, which selects random numbers from a range that you specify. This can be really useful when you want to move a sprite or a pen around the screen.

Enter the code from the screenshot below:

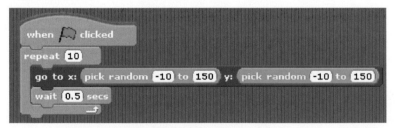

Now add the code from the screenshot on the right to draw the sprite's random path. You might want to shrink your sprite so that you can see the path it draws more clearly.

Activities

26 Write a program to move your sprite across the entire screen at random and draw a colourful path as it does so. Shrink your sprite to a small dot, then enter the code from the screenshot below and run it.

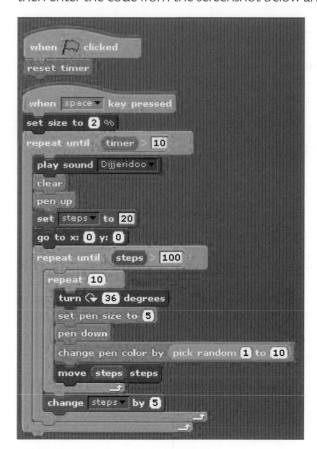

Your screen should look like the screenshot below:

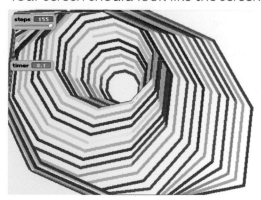

27 Write a program.
- Create a pattern using a decagon.
- The decagon should increase its size as it moves around the screen until it reaches a maximum of 150 steps.
- It should then stop, play a sound and output a message using a sprite.
- It should use a timer to record the length of time it takes to make the pattern.
- If the pattern takes more than 20 seconds it should output a suitable message.

Chapter 3

Implementation (Visual Basic)

What you should know

By the end of this chapter you should **know** and **understand** how to use the Visual Basic development environment to implement:

★ the five data types required at National 5 level – character, string, numeric (integer and real) and Boolean

★ the two data structures required at National 5 level – variables and one-dimensional arrays

★ the following constructs:

  ★ expressions to assign values
  ★ expressions to return values using arithmetic operations (addition, subtraction, multiplication, division and exponentiation)
  ★ expressions to concatenate strings
  ★ selection constructs using simple conditional statements with <, >, ≤, ≥, =, ≠ operators
  ★ selection constructs using complex conditional statements
  ★ logical operators (AND, OR, NOT)
  ★ iteration and repetition using fixed and conditional loops
  ★ predefined functions (with parameters):
    ★ random
    ★ round
    ★ length

★ the following standard algorithms:

  ★ input validation
  ★ running total within loop
  ★ traversing a one-dimensional array.

Visual Basic introduction

Step 1 Getting started

Your teacher will help you open Visual Basic and make sure that the *standard* toolbar is showing by using the *view* and *toolbar* menus.

Now select Windows Application and give it a name as shown in the screenshot:

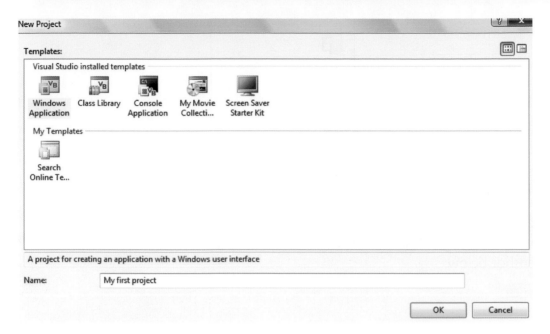

The *form* window will appear as shown in the screenshot below. This is where you will design your program.

Step 2 Finding out about the toolbox

Your screen has a toolbox (see right margin) which is very important. Click on it to open it. It has lots of tools; don't worry, you are only going to use a few of them to start with. The ones you will mainly use will be:

- the *button* tool
- the *label* tool
- the *textbox* tool
- and, later on, the *listbox* tool.

You will need to use the following icons:

New Project icon (that you have already seen)	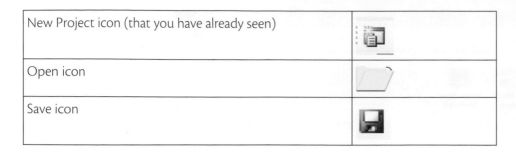
Open icon	
Save icon	

Step 3 Using a button

Open the toolbox and drag a button onto your form. You can change the shape of your button by dragging the handles. Your form should look something like the screenshot below:

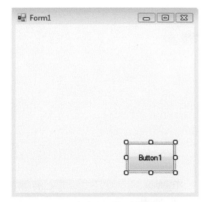

You should now change the text on the button to Start. To do this you need to go to the *properties* window, which is on the right-hand side of your screen.

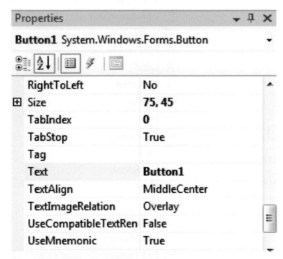

Click on the text Button1 and change it to Start as on the screenshot below:

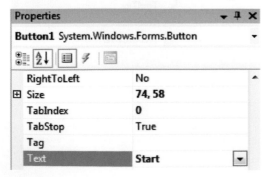

Your button should now look like the screenshot below:

Step 4 Entering your first program code

Now double click on your *start* button and the window will open to allow you to put in your program code. The code you will put in will be:

```
MsgBox("My first VB program by my name")
```

Be careful to type it in correctly, making sure you enter the brackets ( ) and the " ".

Note: You should put in your own name!

This code will open up a message box on the screen and print the text in between the brackets and speech marks (" ") as shown in the screenshot below.

```
Public Class Form1

    Private Sub Button1_Click(ByVal sender As System

        MsgBox(" My first VB program by my name")

    End Sub
End Class
```

Step 5 Testing your program

Now test your program by clicking on the *run* icon at the top of the screen, which is shown in the screenshot to the right.

Now click on the *start* button and, if there are no errors, your screen will look like the screenshot below:

Click on OK and the message box will go away. Now stop your program running by clicking on the stop icon (see screenshot to the right) at the top of the screen.

Step 6 Saving your program

Now save your program by opening the *file* menu and selecting Save All as shown in the screenshot on the right:

Now name your project *first project* and click on Save as shown in the screenshot below:

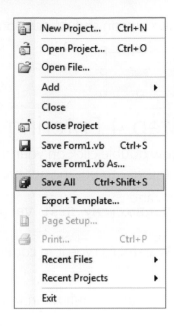

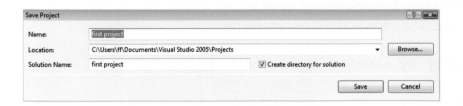

You have now completed your first VB project!

Activities

1 Print your school name using a message box. Save it as Visual Basic Activity 1.
2 Print your address using a message box. Save it as Visual Basic Activity 2.
3 Print your favourite pop star's name using a message box. Save it as Visual Basic Activity 3.

Step 7 Accepting numbers into your program

In this section you are going to learn how to get whole numbers into your program. In Visual Basic we call a whole number an integer. To get a number in, we are going to use an input box that will appear on the screen. Input boxes are used to allow a user to enter data, as shown in the screenshot below:

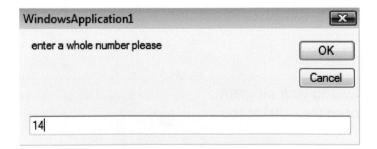

We will use the code:

```
Inputbox("Enter a whole number please")
```

But we will need to put the number that is entered into a box in the computer's memory. We call these boxes variables. So we will have to set up a box called *number* using this line of code:

```
Dim number As Integer
```

This sets up a box in the computer's memory called *number*.

Now you have to tell the computer to take the number from the input box and put it into the number box using this line of code:

```
number = Inputbox("Enter a whole number please")
```

We can then tell the computer to use a message box to put a message, and whatever is in the number box, on the screen using this line of code:

```
MsgBox("The number you entered was" & number)
```

Now let's get started by opening up a new form by following Step 1 again. This time call your new project *Integer example*. Now add a button and change its text to Start, following Step 3.

Now double click on the *start* button to open your *coding* window and enter your code. Your screen should look like the screenshot below:

```
Public Class Form1

    Private Sub Button1_Click(ByVal sender As System.Object, ByVal

        Dim number As Integer
        number = InputBox("enter a whole number please ")
        MsgBox("You entered the whole number " & number)

    End Sub
End Class
```

Test

Now test your program by clicking on the *run* icon. If there are no errors then the input box will ask you to enter a number and the message box will display the number on the screen as shown in the screenshot below:

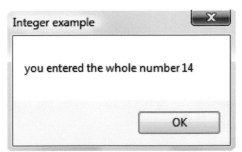

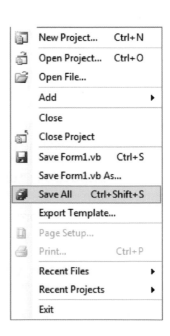

Don't forget to stop the program running by clicking on the *stop* icon.

Now save your project as *Integer example* by selecting Save All from the *file* menu as shown in the screenshot on the right.

Activities

4 Write a program that asks for and displays the number of people in your family. Save it as Visual Basic Activity 4.

5 Write a program that asks for and displays the number of hours you watch television each day. Save it as Visual Basic Activity 5.

Remember

Variables are boxes in the computer's memory that you use to store, for example, numbers or words.

So far you have only used a variable to hold a whole number like 1, 2, 3 and so on, but you can store decimal numbers, for example, 1.25, 2.34, 20.45.

Here are the different types of variables that you will use:

Type	Coding	What it can hold	Example
Character	Dim letter as Char	One key from the keyboard	a
String	Dim name as String	A sequence of characters	Fred
Integer	Dim whole_number as Integer	Numbers without a fraction	14
Real	Dim decimal_number as Single	Decimal numbers (fractions)	16.75
Boolean	Dim finished as Boolean	True or False	True

Step 8 Accepting words into your program

To get a name in, you are going to use an input box which will appear on the screen. You will use the code:

```
InputBox("Enter a name please")
```

But we will need to put the name that is entered into a box in the computer's memory. We call these boxes variables. So we will have to set up a box called *name* using this line of code:

```
Dim name As String
```

Now you have to tell the computer to take the name from the input box and put it into the name box using this line of code:

```
name = InputBox("Enter a name please")
```

We can then tell the computer to use a message box to put a message, and whatever is in the name box, on the screen using this line of code:

```
MsgBox("The name you entered was" & name)
```

Now let's get started by opening up a new form by following Step 1 again. Just as you did for numbers, open up a new project and call it *Name example.*

Now add a button to your form and change its text to Start, just as you did in Step 3 on pages 30–31.

Your form should look like the screenshot below:

```
Public Class Form1

    Private Sub Button1_Click(ByVal sender As System.Object,

        Dim name As String

        name = InputBox(" enter a name please")

        MsgBox("The name you entered was " & name)

    End Sub
End Class
```

Now double click on the *start* button and enter the code for your program so that it looks like the screenshot below:

Test

Now test your program by clicking on the *run* icon. If there are no errors then the input box will ask you to enter a name and the message box will display the name on the screen as in the screenshot below:

Now save your project as *name example* by selecting Save All from the *file* menu.

Activities

6　Write a program that asks for and displays the title of a song. Save it as Visual Basic Activity 6.

7　Write a program that asks for and displays the name of a book. Save it as Visual Basic Activity 7.

Step 9 Accepting words into your program

Now you are going to write a program that will input words and numbers and display them on the screen. Open a new project and call it *Words and numbers*. Put a start button on your form. Now enter the code that follows to input the name of a pop star and give them a rating number between 1 and 5.

```
Dim Pop_star_name As String
Dim rating As Integer
Pop_star_name = InputBox("Enter the name of a pop star please")
rating = InputBox("Give your pop star a rating between 1 and 5. 1 is the
best and 5 the worst.")
MsgBox("Your pop star you entered was " & Pop_star_name)
MsgBox("The rating you gave was " & rating)
```

Your coding should look like this:

```
Public Class Form1
    Private Sub Button1_Click(ByVal sender As System.Object, ByVal e As
    System.EventArgs) Handles Button1.Click
        Dim Pop_star_name As String
        Dim rating As Integer
        Pop_star_name = InputBox("Enter the name of a pop star please")
        rating = InputBox("Give your pop star a rating between 1 and 5. 1
        is the best and 5 the worst.")
        MsgBox("Your pop star you entered was " & Pop_star_name)
        MsgBox("The rating you gave was " & rating)
    End Sub
End Class
```

Note: If you want to use a variable name with two or more words, you have to use the underscore like this:

```
Pop_Star_Name
```

You can't use *Pop Star Name*, as Visual Basic won't accept spaces in a variable name.

Test

Now test your program using the *run* icon.

Don't forget to stop the program running by clicking on the *stop* icon. Save your program as *Names and numbers*.

Note: From now on you should place comments in your program explaining who wrote it, when it was written and what the program does.

```
' Program to ask for song and position in charts
' By Ali Mac
' May 2013
' Saved as 'Name and Age'
```

Note: You have to start a comment by using '.

Activities

8   Write a program that asks for and displays the title of a song and its position in the charts. Save it as Visual Basic Activity 8.

9   Write a program that asks for and displays your name and your age. Save it as Visual Basic Activity 9.

Step 10 Adding up numbers

You are now going to write a program to add up some numbers.

Open a new project. Call it *Adding up*. On your form place a button and change its text to *Add numbers* as shown in the screenshot on the right:

Double click on the *Add numbers* button to open up the window for your coding.

First you need to set up the boxes (the variables) to store the numbers:

```
Dim cd_cost As Integer
Dim dvd_cost As Integer
Dim total_cost As Integer
```

Now you need to enter the code to input the costs:

```
cd_cost = InputBox("Enter the cost of a CD in pence please")
dvd_cost = InputBox("Enter the cost of a DVD in pence please")
```

Next add the code to add up the two costs to give the total cost:

```
total_cost = cd_cost + dvd_cost
```

Lastly, use a message box to display the total cost to the screen:

```
MsgBox("The total cost in pence = " & total_cost)
```

Your screen should now look like this:

```
Public Class Form1
    Private Sub Button1_Click(ByVal sender As System.Object, ByVal e As
    System.EventArgs) Handles Button1.Click
        Dim cd_cost As Integer
        Dim dvd_cost As Integer
        Dim total_cost As Integer
        cd_cost = InputBox("Enter the cost of a CD in pence please")
        dvd_cost = InputBox("Enter the cost of a DVD in pence please")
        total_cost = dvd_cost
        MsgBox("The total cost in pence = " & total_cost)
    End Sub
End Class
```

Now test your program using the *run* icon. Don't forget to stop the program running by clicking on the *stop* icon. Save your program as *adding up*.

Adding, subtracting, multiplying, dividing, power of

You have used the + sign for adding up. You need to know how to subtract, multiply and divide. Use this table to help you.

Adding	+
Subtracting	–
Multiplying	*
Dividing	/
Power of	^

Activities

10 Write a program to add up the cost of two computer games and display the total.
   ● Draw a structure diagram for this program.
   ● Then write the program.
   Save it as Visual Basic Activity 10.

11 Write a program to add up the cost of two films on DVD and display the total.
   ● Draw a structure diagram for this program.
   ● Then write the program.
   Save it as Visual Basic Activity 11.

Activity

12 Write a program to:

a) enter the names and cost in pence of each of the following grocery items:

Honey	230
Salmon	198
Nuts	125
Tea	240
Eggs	175

b) display the total cost of all of the items.

c) calculate and display your change from £10.

The output from your program should look something like the screenshot on the right:

You need to complete a report for Activity 12. The report should contain:

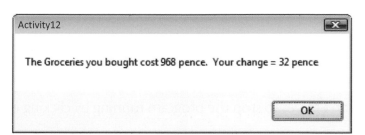

- a description of the task
- your structure diagram
- the test data you have been given (the list of groceries and costs).

You should ask your teacher to check:

- your report
- your coding
- your test run.

Step 11 Using a fixed loop

In programming we use *loops* to repeat actions over and over again.

Open a new form as shown in the screenshot on the right:

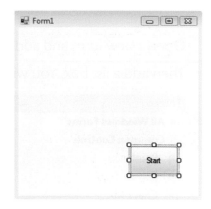

Place a *start* button on the form, click on the button and enter the coding below:

```
Dim counter As Integer
Dim name As String
For counter = 1 To 5
        name = Inputbox("Enter the name of a pupil in your class please")
    Msgbox("The name you entered was " & name)
Next
```

The program will go round the loop five times, taking in a name each time and displaying it in a message box.

Your form should look like this:

```
Public Class Form1
    Private Sub Button1_Click(ByVal sender As System.Object, ByVal e As
    System.EventArgs) Handles Button1.Click
        Dim counter As Integer
        Dim name As String
        For counter = 1 To 5
            name = InputBox("Enter the name of a pupil in your class please")
            MsgBox("The name you entered was " & name)
        Next
    End Sub
End Class
```

Now test your program using the *run* icon. Your program should ask you five times for the name of a pupil in your class then display it!

Don't forget to stop the program running by clicking on the *stop* icon.

Save your program as *For Next1*.

Step 12 Using a loop with a listbox

You use listboxes when you want to display lists of names or numbers, for example.

Open a new form and add a button. Change its text to read *Enter Names*.

Then add a list box. You will find it in your toolbox:

Go to the *properties* window and change the name of the listbox to *Names_list* as shown on the screenshot on the right:

Your form should now look like the screenshot below:

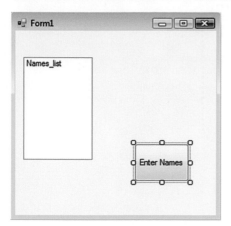

Now click on the *Enter Names* button and add this coding:

```
Public Class Form1
    Private Sub Button1_Click(ByVal sender As System.Object, ByVal e As
    System.EventArgs) Handles Button1.Click
        Dim counter As Integer
        Dim name As String
        For counter = 1 To 5
            name = InputBox("Enter the name of a pupil in your class please")
            Names_list.Items.Add(name)
        Next
    End Sub
End Class
```

Now test your program using the *run* icon.

Your program should ask you five times for the name of a pupil in your class then display it in the listbox as shown on the screenshot below.

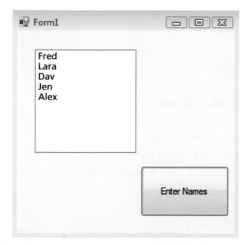

Don't forget to stop the program running by clicking on the *stop* icon.
Save your program as *For Next listbox*.

 **Activity**

13 Write a program to enter and display the names of five of your favourite pop stars.
- Draw a structure diagram for this program.
- Then write the program.

Save it as Visual Basic Activity 13.

Step 13 Using a loop and a listbox to display names and numbers

Open a new form and add a button. Change its text to read *Enter Teams and Goals*.

Then add a listbox and change its name to *teamslist*.

Your form should now look like the screenshot below:

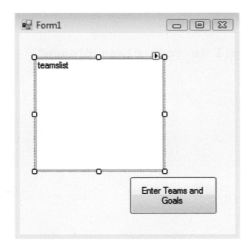

Now click on the *Enter Teams and Goals* button and add the coding below:

```
Public Class Form1
    Private Sub Button1_Click(ByVal sender As System.Object, ByVal e As
    System.EventArgs) Handles Button1.Click
        Dim team As String ' this holds the name of the team
        Dim goals As Integer ' this holds the number of goals
        Dim counter As Integer ' this counts the number of times around
        the loop
        For counter = 1 To 5
            team = InputBox("Enter the name of a team")
            goals = InputBox("Enter the goals for the team")
            teamslist.Items.Add(team & " " & goals)
        Next
    End Sub
End Class
```

Note: Ensure this time you have added comments to explain what is going on in your program.

Remember

Comments start with a '. For example:

' this holds the name of the team

Comments are coloured green!

Now test your program using the *run* icon.

Your form should look something like the screenshot below.

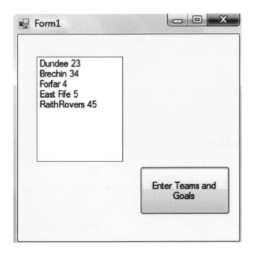

Don't forget to stop the program running by clicking on the stop icon.
Save your program as *Teams and Goals*.

14 Write a program to enter and display the names of five of your
    school subjects and marks out of 100.
    ● Draw a structure diagram for this program.
    ● Then write the program.
    Save it as Visual Basic Activity 14.

Step 14 Running total within a loop and working out an average

Open up your *Teams and Goals* program and make the changes below to
calculate the average number of goals.

You need to set up a variable to hold the total goals and one to hold the average.

```
Dim Total_goals As Integer
Dim Average As Integer
```

Inside the loop add this coding to calculate the total:

```
Total_goals= Total_goals + Goals
```

Outside the loop add this coding to calculate the average:

```
Average = Total_goals/5
```

Use a message box to output the average by adding this code *outside the loop*:

```
MsgBox = ("The average = " & Average)
```

Your form should now look like this:

```
Public Class Form1
    Private Sub Button1_Click(ByVal sender As System.Object, ByVal e As
    System.EventArgs) Handles Button1.Click
        ' A program using a for next loop and a listbox
        ' By Name D Onut
        Dim Team As String ' this holds the name of the team
        Dim Goals As Integer ' this holds the number of goals
        Dim counter As Integer ' this counts the number of times around
        the loop
        Dim Total_goals As Integer
        Dim Average As Integer
        For counter = 1 To 5
            Team = InputBox("Enter the name of a team")
            Goals = InputBox("Enter the goals for the team ")
            teamslist.Items.Add(Team & " " & Goals)
            Total_goals = Total_goals + Goals
        Next
        Average = Total_goals / 5
        MsgBox("The average = " & Average)
    End Sub
End Class
```

Now test your program using the *run* icon.

Your output should look something like the screenshots below:

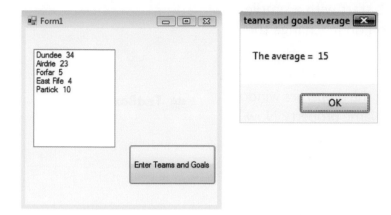

Don't forget to stop the program running by clicking on the stop icon.
Save your program as *Teams and Goals Average*.

15 Write a program that:
   ● inputs and displays the names and costs of five smartphones in a list
   ● displays the average cost of the phones.

You need to complete a report for Activity 15. The report should contain:
● a description of the task
● your structure diagram
● your test data.

You should ask your teacher to check:
● your report
● your coding
● your test run.

Using textboxes

So far when we have been inputting data we have used an input box. You can also use a textbox to enter data. Let's start with a simple example. Open a new form and place a button on it. Change the button's text to *Get message.*

Next go to your toolbox and place a textbox on your form. You are now going to give your textbox a suitable name using the *properties* window. Scroll up the *properties* window till you see the Name property. Now change it from *TextBox1* to *Read_number.*

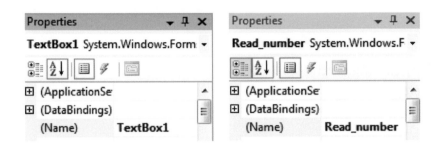

Now you need to add a label so that you know what the textbox is for. Go to your toolbox and drag a label onto your form and then change its text to read *Enter number.*

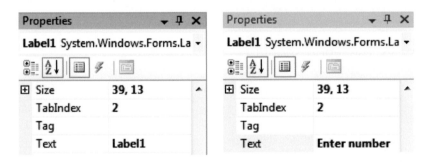

Your form should look something like the screenshot below:

Now to enter the coding click on the *Get message* button, or click on the *form tab*.

Enter the coding below:

```
Dim number As Integer
number = Read_number.Text
MsgBox("The number you entered was " & number)
```

Your coding should look like this:

```
Public Class Form1
    Private Sub Button1_Click(ByVal sender As System.Object, ByVal e As
    System.EventArgs) Handles Button1.Click
        Dim number As Integer
        number = Read_number.Text
        MsgBox("The number you entered was " & number)
    End Sub
End Class
```

Something is missing. Can you guess what it is? It is the comment lines.
- Add your own details at the start, for example:

```
' Program to XXXXXXXX
' By XXXXXX
' Date XXXXX
' Saved as XXXXXXXX
```

- Add a few comment lines explaining what your program does.
- Test your program using the *run* icon.

Your form should look something like the screenshot below:

When you press the *Get message* button, a message box like the one in the screenshot below should appear:

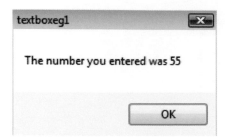

Don't forget to stop the program running by clicking on the *stop* icon.

Save your program as *textboxeg1*.

Note: Textboxes can also be used to display data that is used inside the program. You will see this later when we use textboxes to display numbers.

Using a textbox and an *If*

You can use an *If* to get your program to make a decision. For example, your program can decide if a number is too big.

Open the program *textboxeg1* you just completed. Add the coding below:

```
If number > 50 Then
    MsgBox("The number you entered was greater than 50")
End If
```

Your coding should now look like this:

```
Public Class Form1
    Private Sub Button1_Click(ByVal sender As System.Object, ByVal e As
    System.EventArgs) Handles Button1.Click
            Dim number As Integer
            number = Read_number.Text
            MsgBox("The number you entered was " & number)
            If number > 50 Then
              MsgBox("The number you entered was greater than 50")
        End If
    End Sub
End Class
```

Now test your program using the *run* icon. Enter any number greater than 50, for example 55. When you press the *Get message* button a message box like this should appear:

When you click on the *OK* button another message box like this should appear:

Don't forget to stop the program running by clicking on the *stop* icon.

Save your program as *Ifexample1*.

You used > to check if something was *greater than* something else. You need to know all the operators used for making comparisons:

Greater than	>
Less than	<
Equals	=
Greater that or equal to	>=
Less than or equal to	<=
Does not equal	<>

Activities

16 Write a program that asks for the cost of a laptop computer. If the cost is greater than 200 then a suitable message should be output. Save your program as Visual Basic Activity 16.

17 Write a program to check a password. If the password is not correct then a message should be displayed refusing authorisation. Save your program as Visual Basic Activity 17.

18 Write a program that:
- takes in the names and marks out of 100 for 10 pupils
- displays the names and marks
- counts up how many pass (the pass mark is 50)
- displays the number of passes.

You need to complete a report for Activity 18. The report should contain:
- a description of the task
- your structure diagram
- your test data.

You should ask your teacher to check:
- your report
- your coding
- your test run

Formatting numbers

You will need to change the way that numbers appear on your screen in some programs. Check out this example:

Open up a form and add a button with the text *Format a number* and three text boxes, each with a label as shown in the screenshot below:

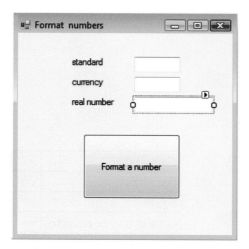

The textboxes in this program will be used to display data being used in the program.

Click on the button and enter the following text:

```
Dim number As Single
number = 45.6789
TextBox1.Text = Format(number, "standard")
TextBox2.Text = Format(number, "currency")
TextBox3.Text = Format(number, "general number")
MsgBox("The total cost is " & Format(number, "standard"))
MsgBox("The total cost is " & Format(number, "currency"))
MsgBox("The total cost is " & Format(number, "general number"))
```

Now test the program. It should look like the screenshot below:

Remember

Formatting numbers

Format(number, "standard")	gives a number to two decimal places	45.68
Format(number, "currency")	gives a £ sign	£45.68
Format(number, "general number")	gives a number with lots of decimal places	45.67890167

Controlling a loop

You have used fixed loops to get your programs to repeat actions, for example:

```
Dim counter As Integer
For counter = 1 To 5
     ListBox1.Items.Add("My High School")
Next
```

This code will repeat the words *My High School* five times in a listbox as shown in the screenshot below.

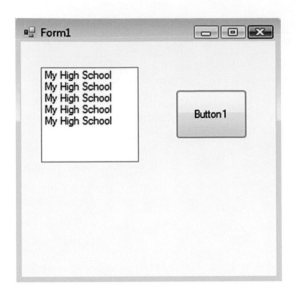

Now you are going to use a variable to let the user decide how many times the program will go round the loop.

Open a new project, add a *start* button then add the coding below:

```
' Program to XXXXXXXXX
' By XXXXXX
' Date XXXXX
' Saved as XXXXXXXX
Dim number As Integer
Dim price As Integer
Dim total As Integer
Dim counter As Integer
price = InputBox("Enter the price of a computer game in pounds") ' this
takes in the price set by the user
number = InputBox("Enter the number of games you want to buy") this takes
in the number of games the user wants
For counter = 1 To number ' uses the number variable to control the loop
total = total + price ' adds a price to the total each time round the loop
Next
    MsgBox("The total cost of your games is £" & total) ' this displays
    the total
```

This program uses the variable *number* to control the number of times round the *for…next loop*.

Test your program then save it as *Control Loop*.

Activities

19 Write a program that:
   a) asks for the number of pens a pupil wants
   b) asks for the price of a pen
   c) displays the total costs of the pens.
   Save your program as Visual Basic Activity 19.

20 Write a program that:
   a) asks for the number of books that a school wants to order
   b) asks for the price of a book
   c) displays the total costs of the books.
   Save your program as Visual Basic Activity 20.

Conditional loops

So far you have used *For…Next* loops to repeat actions in your programs.

Now you are going to use loops that are controlled by using conditions (conditional loops).

You are going to use *Do…loop until*.

Using *Do…loop until*

This program will ask the user to enter a number and then adds up the total until the total is greater than 100. The program will display the total as it goes along.

Pseudocode

1   Initialise

2   Loop enter numbers until total is greater than 100

1.1 Setup number as an integer

1.2 Setup total as an integer

2.1 Start loop
        2.1 Prompt for number
        2.2 Input number
        2.3 Add number to total
        2.4 Display total

2.5 Until total is greater than 100

****

Now:
● Open a new project.
● Add a start button.
● Add a textbox to your form.

- Change the textbox's name to output_total as shown in the screenshot on the right:

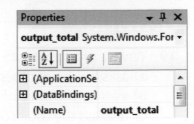

Now add a *label* to explain what the textbox is used for as shown in the screenshot below:

Tag	
Text	**running total**
TextAlign	TopLeft

Your form should now look like the screenshot below:

Now click on your *start* button and add the following code:

```
Dim number As Integer
Dim total As Integer
Do
     number = InputBox("Enter a number please ")
     total = total + number ' adds a number to the total
     output_total.Text = total ' displays the total in the textbox
Loop Until total > 100 ' sets the condition: a total greater than 100
```

Your program should keep on asking for a number and changing the running total until it is greater than 100 as in the screenshot below.

Save your program as *Do loop until example*.

This program is an example of a running total within a loop.

Activities

21 Write a program that asks for and adds up the total number of tickets sold until the total is greater than 50.
   Don't forget to produce the pseudocode for this program.
   Save your program as Visual Basic Activity 21.

22 Write a program that keeps asking for a password until it is correct.
   Don't forget to produce the pseudocode for this program.
   Save your program as Visual Basic Activity 22.

23 Write a program that asks for a PIN (Personal Identity Number).
   ● If the PIN entered is '4848' then a 'correct' message should be displayed.
   ● If the PIN entered is not '4848' then an error message should be displayed and the user should be asked to enter the PIN again.
   ● The program should repeat this process until the correct PIN is entered.

You need to complete a report for Activity 23. The report should contain:
● a description of the task
● your structure diagram
● your test data.

You should ask your teacher to check:
● your report
● your coding
● your test run.

Using *Do...loop until* with a complex condition

This program will ask the user to enter a number, then adds up the total until the total is greater than 100 and less than 200. The program will display the total as it goes along.

Pseudocode

1. Initialise

2. Loop and enter numbers until total is greater than 100 and less than 200

1.1 setup number as an integer

1.2 setup total as an integer

2.1 start loop
     2.1 prompt for number
     2.2 input number
     2.3 add number to total
     2.4 display total

2.5 until total is greater than 100 and less than 200

****

Open your saved *Do…loop until example.*

Now add the following complex condition to the end of the loop:

```
Loop Until total > 100 and total < 200 ' This is a complex condition
```

Your code should now look like this:

```
Dim number As Integer
Dim total As Integer
Do
    number = InputBox("Enter a number please ")
    total = total + number ' adds a number to the total
    output_total.Text = total ' displays the total in the textbox
Loop Until total > 100 and total < 200 ' This is a complex condition
```

Your program should keep on asking for a number and changing the running total until it is greater than 100 and less than 200 as in the screenshot below.

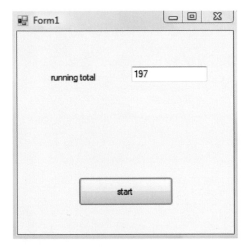

Save your program as *Do loop until example.*

 Activity

24 Write a program that asks for and adds up the total number of tickets sold until the total is greater than 50 and less than 80. Don't forget to produce the pseudocode for this program. Save your program as Visual Basic Activity 24.

Input validation using a *Do while…loop*

When you used the *Do…loop until*, the condition was at the end of the loop:

```
Do
    number = InputBox("Enter a number please ")
    total = total + number
    output_total.Text = total
Loop Until total > 100 and total <200 ' the condition is at the end of the
loop
```

When you use a *Do while ... loop* the condition is at the start of a loop:

```
Do While mark < 0
     mark= InputBox("Out of range, please enter a mark greater than 0")
Loop
```

This coding is using the *Do while...loop* to check that a mark being entered is greater than 0, a simple condition!

You will now write a program that will check that marks being entered are greater than −1 and less than 101. This is a complex condition with two parts to the condition: *greater than −1 and less than 101*.

- Start a new project.
- Add a button and change its text to *Average 5 Marks*.
- Add a textbox to hold the total of the five marks. Change its name to *Total_marks*. Give it a label with the same text.
- Add another textbox to hold the average mark. Change its name to *Average_mark*. Give it a label with the same name.

Your form should now look similar to the screenshot below:

Now add the following code to your button:

```
' Program to XXXXXXXXX
' By XXXXXX
' Date XXXXX
' Saved as XXXXXXXX
Dim mark As Integer
Dim counter As Integer
Dim total As Integer
Dim average As Single ' note this can store numbers with decimal points
   For counter = 1 To 5
     mark = InputBox("Enter a mark between 0 and 100 ")
        Do While mark < 0 Or mark > 100 ' this holds a complex condition
          mark = InputBox("Out of range. Please enter a mark between 0 and
          100 ") ' this asks for another mark within the range
Loop
total = total + mark 'this adds up the marks using a running total
Total_marks.Text = total 'this puts the total into the Total_marks box
Next
   average = total / 5
   Average_mark.Text = average 'this puts the average into the Average_marks box
```

Test data

Now test your program by putting in a range of numbers that check whether or not marks below 0 or above 100 will be accepted.

You should include the numbers −1 and 101 as part of your test data.

Activity

25   Open a Word file and copy and complete this test data table:

Normal Test Data	Expected Result	Actual Result
23	mark accepted	
48	mark accepted	
75		
93		
Extreme Test Data	**Expected Result**	**Actual Result**
100	mark accepted	
0		
Exceptional Test Data	**Expected Result**	**Actual Result**
−1	out of range	
101	out of range	
2134		
897		
345.78		

If you enter a number that is out of range, you should get an error message as shown in the screenshot below:

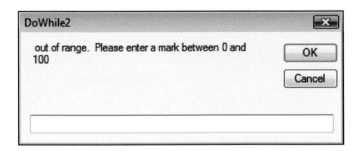

Once you have entered five valid numbers, your form should look something like the screenshot on the right:

Save your program as *Do while example*.

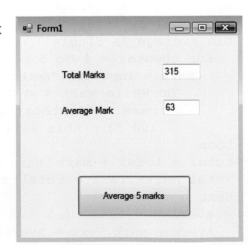

Activity

26 Write a program that:
- asks the user to enter the cost of five different DVD movies (the maximum cost should be 14.99 and the minimum 5.50)
- calculates and displays the average cost of a DVD.

Save it as Visual Basic Activity 26.

You must:
- produce the pseudocode for this program
- produce a test data table for this program and complete it as you test the program.

Complex conditions

In the *Do while…* example above, you used a complex condition to check whether the mark was between 0 and 100.

When you use complex conditions you use one of the following operators: AND, OR, NOT

Operator	What it does
AND	Using *AND* joins two conditions together, for example: *If name ="Fred" AND ID = "Fr1234" then…* both conditions must be met before the *If* is satisfied.
OR	Using an *OR* means that only one of the conditions needs to be met, for example: *If price < 0 OR price > 30 then…*
NOT	Using *NOT* negates a result, for example: *IF NOT (number = 50) then…* If the conditional expression is false, then the result is true. If the conditional expression is true, then the result is false.

Activity

27 Write a program that:
- asks the user for their customer number
- gives an acceptance message if their customer number is greater than 0 and less than 1000.

You must produce the pseudocode for this program.

Save it as Visual Basic Activity 27.

If...then...else

You can use *If...then...else* to let your program decide two options. Enter the simple example below that checks a PIN number using a start button:

```
Dim pin_number As Integer
pin_number = 1234
    If pin_number = InputBox("Enter your PIN number please ") Then
    MsgBox("correct")
    Else : MsgBox("Wrong PIN number")
End If
```

Activity

28 Write a program that checks the name of your favourite pop star. If the wrong name is entered then the program should display a suitable error message.
Save it as Visual Basic Activity 28.

If...then...elseif...elseif...else end if

You can use *If...then...elseif...elseif...else end if* to allow your program to select between a range of options.

Try out this simple example:

```
Dim name As String
Dim comment As String
name = InputBox("Enter a name")
    If name = "Jack" Then
        comment = "Hi Jack"
    ElseIf name = "Mack" Then
        comment = "Hi Mack"
    ElseIf name = "Ed" Then
        comment = "Hi Ed"
    Else
        comment = "Who are you?"
    End If
    MsgBox(comment)
```

An alternative way of checking a multiple choice is to use a *CASE*:

```
Dim name As String
name = InputBox("Enter a name")
Select Case name
    Case Is = "Jack"
        MsgBox("Hi Jack")
    Case Is = "Mack"
        MsgBox("Hi Mack")
    Case Else
        MsgBox("Who are you?")
End Select
```

Activity

29 Write a program to process five pupils' exam marks. The program should:

- take in five pupils' names and exam marks
- display each pupil's name, mark and their grade.

The grades must be awarded as follows:

Marks out of 100	Award
70–100	A
60–69	B
50–59	C
<50	D

You should supply your own test data table designed to make sure that the grading is done accurately.

You need to complete a report for Activity 29. The report should contain:

- a description of the task
- your pseudocode
- a table with test data that you have produced.

You should ask your teacher to check:

- your report
- your coding
- your test run and test data table.

Using checkboxes

Checkboxes are an easy way to enter a user's selections into your form. Let's look at this example that uses checkboxes to make up a pizza.

- Start a new project.
- Add a button and change its text to *Show toppings chosen*.
- Add three checkboxes within and change each of their texts in turn to *Peppers*, *Cheese* and *Mushrooms*.
- Add labels to each checkbox with the text *Peppers*, *Cheese* and *Mushrooms*.
- Add a listbox and change its name to *Pizza*. Give it a label *Pizza toppings*.

Your form should look like this:

Now click on the button and add the following code:

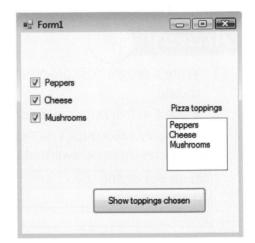

```
If CheckBox1.Checked = True Then
     Pizza.Items.Add(CheckBox1.Text)
End If
If CheckBox2.Checked = True Then
     Pizza.Items.Add(CheckBox2.Text)
End If
If CheckBox2.Checked = True Then
     Pizza.Items.Add(CheckBox3.Text)
End If
```

This adds the text attached to the checkbox into the listbox if the checkbox is ticked.

Test your program. Your form should look something like the screenshot on the right:

Activity

30 Write a program that:
- uses checkboxes to select four smartphones from a list of five
- stores their costs in an array
- displays the individual costs and total cost of the four phones.

Nofia v6	£60.99
Blueberry Super5	£90.00
BearPhone V3	£20.34
Gibber V5	£50.89
TeaMobil	£67.45

Save it as Visual Basic Activity 30.

Combobox

A combobox provides the user with a dropdown menu from which they can choose *one* item.

Comboboxes are useful when you want to give the user a limited choice.

The user's selection from a combobox is read as text.

Here a combobox is being used to find out the number of items being ordered and checkboxes to get the customer's choice of item.

This example uses a combobox to input the number of the customer's order. Use a combobox + label, two checkboxes, a textbox + label and a button to calculate the total cost depending on the user's selection.

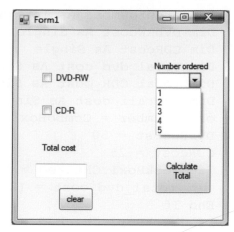

Filling the combobox

When you have inserted your combobox, you need to fill it with the numbers 1, 2, 3, 4, 5, which will be shown to the user. Follow these steps:

- Click on the combobox.
- Select the item's property.
- Click on the collection tab.

A window will open up in which you enter the numbers you want to display, one number on each line as shown in the screenshot below.

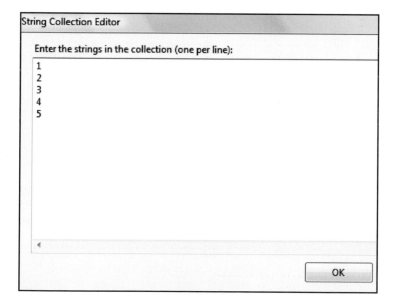

The coding is given below:

```
Dim ordernumber As Integer
Dim DVDRWcost As Single
Dim CDRcost As Single
Dim total_dvd_cost As Single
Dim total_CDR_cost As Single
Dim Overall_cost As Single
ordernumber = ComboBox1.Text
DVDRWcost = 50
CDRcost = 25
If CheckBox1.Checked = True Then
     total_dvd_cost = (DVDRWcost * ordernumber)
End If
If CheckBox2.Checked = True Then
     total_CDR_cost = (CDRcost * ordernumber)
End If
Overall_cost = total_dvd_cost + total_CDR_cost
     Totalbox.Text = Overall_cost
```

Note: You can use *if…elseif…end if* to get the same result.

Save your program as *Comboexample*.

Activities

31 Write a program using a combobox to enter and display the user's choice of song to download.
    You must produce the pseudocode for this program.
    Save it as Visual Basic Activity 31.

32 Write a program to calculate the cost of the air tickets for a family of up to five in number. The cost of tickets is as follows:

Economy seat	£100
Premium seat	£180

The program should enable the user to clear the display of the cost and enter new choices.
You must produce the pseudocode for this program.
Save it as Visual Basic Activity 32.

Using arrays

An array is a list of numbers or words. Each array has a name. This array is called *Name*.

Index	0	1	2	3
Name	Fred	Lara	Dav	Jen

Each array has an index. The index is used to count down (or up) the array.

Note: Visual Basic starts counting from 0.

So *Name(0)* is Fred, *Name(1)* is Lara and so on.

This array is called *Prices*.

Index	0	1	2	3
Prices	34.99	12.50	14.30	56.00

Here *Prices(0)* is 34.99, *Prices(1)* is 12.50 and so on.

Setting up and filling an array

The first thing you have to do is set up your array using the DIM instruction, for example, DIM Name(4) as string.

$$\underset{\text{size}}{\qquad} \underset{\text{type}}{\qquad}$$

This sets up an array called *Name* with **five** spaces that can hold text.

Next you have to use a loop to fill the array:

```
For index = 0 To 4
    Name(index) = InputBox("Enter a name")
Next index
```

Don't forget to set up your index:

```
DIM index As Integer
```

Time to get started!
- Open a new project.
- Add a button to start filling the array.
- Add a listbox to display the names in your array. Call it *Nameslist*.
- Add a label above your listbox. The text of the label should read '*Names*'.

Your form should look like the screenshot below:

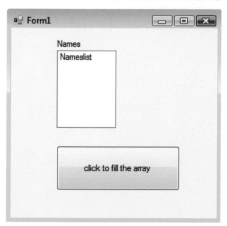

Traversing an array

Example 🚩

Pseudocode

1 Initialise

2 Loop to fill array

3 Loop to display array contents

    1.1 Set up array called name with five spaces

    1.2 Set up index as an integer

    2.1 Start fixed loop for five times

        2.2 Input name into array using index

    2.3 End fixed loop

    3.1 Start fixed loop for five times

        3.2 Display names in array using index

    3.3 End fixed loop

Remember

In Visual Basic, the array begins with the index of 0 for the first entry in the array.

Now add the following code to your button:

```
Dim Name(4) As String ' This sets up the array called name with five spaces
Dim index As Integer
For index = 0 To 4 ' This loop fills the array
    Name(index) = InputBox("Enter a name")
Next index
For index = 0 To 4 ' This loop displays the array in a listbox
    Nameslist.Items.Add(Name(index))
Next index
```

Don't forget to call your listbox *Nameslist*.

Test your program by entering five names.

Your form should look something like the screenshot below:

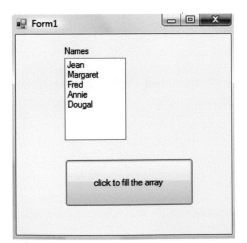

Save your program as *Array1*.

Note: Using one loop to fill the array and another loop to display the names means that the names don't appear in the listbox until you have entered all the names.

Change your program so that the names appear as you type them in. Change the coding to read:

```
Dim name(4) As String
Dim index As Integer
For index = 0 To 4 ' This loop fills the array
    name(index) = InputBox("Enter a name ")
    Nameslist.Items.Add(name(index)) ' This line puts the array contents
    into a listbox
Next index
```

This version only uses one loop and so is more efficient.

Test your program and save it as *Array2*.

Activities

33   Write a program that inputs four names into an array and four whole numbers into an array and displays them, each in their own listbox. You must produce the pseudocode for this program.

Save it as Visual Basic Activity 33.

34   Write a program that:
- inputs four names and four telephone numbers into arrays
- gives the user a choice of 1 to 4
- displays the chosen name and number.

Save it as Visual Basic Activity 34.

Exponentiation

In subjects like physics and maths, you may learn about scientific notation, also known as 'standard form'. This is a way of writing numbers that are very large or very small numbers containing a decimal point. In fact, computers store all real numbers using this format. We call this '**floating point representation**'. You will learn more about how computers store these numbers in Chapter 6.

545 000 000 is a very large number. This would instead be written as 5.45×10^8. The small number, 8, is the exponent. That is because the decimal point has had to move eight places to the left for us to go to 5.45 from 545 000 000. In this example, 5.45 is the mantissa.

If we were writing 0.000926 in this way, it would be written as 9.26×10^{-4}. Here the exponent is −4. This is because the decimal point has had to move four places to the right for us to go to 9.26 from 0.000926. In this example, 9.26 is the mantissa.

In Visual Basic, the '^' symbol is used for 'to the power of'. So, if you needed a program to translate these numbers, you might use a line like:

```
Answer = mantissa × 10 ^ exponent
```

Using pre-defined functions

Functions are code that carries out an operation and then returns a result to your program.

Here are some functions that work with numbers.

The INT and ROUND functions

The INT function takes in a number and gives back the whole number or INTeger part of it. It ignores anything after the decimal point:

- number= INT(3.54) would produce 3
- number= INT(3.14) would produce 3.

The ROUND function will round the numeric value to the nearest whole number:

- number= ROUND(3.54) would produce 4
- number= ROUND(3.14) would produce 3.

You can also specify the number of decimal places to round to by putting this as the second number within the brackets:

- number= ROUND(3.14, 1) would produce 3.1.

Random

This generates a random number.

If you want a random whole number between 0 and 10 then use:

```
DIM RandomNumber as integer
RandomNumber = Rnd() * 10
MsgBox(RandomNumber)
```

For a random number between 0 and 50 change the middle line to:

```
RandomNumber = Rnd() * 50
```

and so on.

Activity

35 Write a program to fill an array with five random numbers between 1 and 100 and display the results in a listbox.
Run your program and then stop. Run it again. What do you notice about the numbers?

Save it as Visual Basic Activity 35.

Note: If you want to repeatedly enter random numbers in your program you have to use the command *Randomise()*.

If you don't use it then the same pattern of numbers will appear again and again.

So your coding would look like this:

```
DIM RandomNumber as integer
Randomise()
    RandomNumber = Rnd() * 10
    MsgBox(RandomNumber)
```

Activity

36 Write a program that will produce a different series of random numbers each time a button is pressed.

Save it as Visual Basic Activity 36.

These functions work with strings:

Name	What it does	Example
Len	Calculates the number of characters in a string	Len("Blob") returns 4
UCase	Converts lowercase characters into uppercase characters	UCase("blob") returns BLOB
LCase	Converts uppercase characters into lowercase characters	LCase("Hello There") returns hello there
Asc	Returns the ASCII value of a character	Asc("A") returns 65
Chr	Takes an ASCII value and returns the corresponding character	Chr(65) returns A
Mid	Extracts a sub-string from a string. It requires three items of data within the brackets, separated by commas. The first is the string to be used, the second is the number of the position of the character to begin the sub-string at, the third is the length of the sub-string in characters	Mid("Word",2,3) returns "ord"

However, the Len function above is the only one of these that is required for the National 5 course.

Activity

37 Try out some examples using your own first name as the string.

- There is some code below to help you.
- Use five buttons to try out the string functions.
- Decide which button each piece of code has to be attached to.

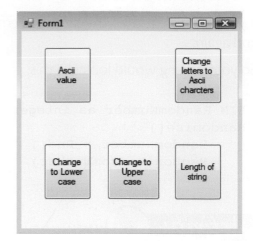

```
Dim Myname As String
Myname = "Fred"
MsgBox("Your name has " & Len(Myname) & " letters")
Dim Myname As String
Myname = "Fred"
MsgBox("Your name has changed from Fred to " & UCase(Myname))
Dim Myname As String
Myname = "Fred"
MsgBox("Your name has changed from Fred to " & LCase(Myname))
MsgBox("The ascii value of letter F is " & Asc("F"))
MsgBox("Number 69 in the Ascii code is letter " & Chr(69))
```

Save it as Visual Basic Activity 37.

Now try this coding out to help you find someone's initials:

```
Dim firstname, secondname As String
Dim initial1, initial2 As String
firstname = InputBox("Enter first name please")
secondname = InputBox("Enter second name please")
initial1 = Mid$(firstname, 1, 1)
initial2 = Mid$(secondname, 1, 1)
MsgBox("Your initials are " & initial1 & " " & initial2)
```

String concatenation

Concatenation is joining two or more strings together to make a completely new string. In Visual Basic this is done using the '+' symbol. This can be done involving only variables, for example:

```
newStr = str1 + str2
```

or also using text within quotes, for example:

```
greeting = "Welcome, " + forename + " " + surname + "."
```

Activities

38 Write a program to make and display a username for someone which combines the first three letters of each of their first name and their second name.
The program will then test the username has been entered correctly before allowing the user to order CDs and display the total cost. Save it as Visual Basic Activity 38.

39 Write a program to:
- store the names and costs of five movie DVDs
- ask for the name of a movie DVD on the list and display the name and price
- display an error message if the movie requested by the user is not on the list!

You need to complete a report for Actvity 39. The report should contain:
- a description of the task
- your pseudocode
- a table with test data that you have produced.

You should ask your teacher to check:
- your report
- your coding
- your test run and test data table.

You have now finished your National 5 Visual Basic Programming.

Chapter 4

Implementation (reading and interpreting code)

What you should know

By the end of this chapter you should **know** and **understand** how to recognise and:

★ identify the five data types required at National 5 level – character, string, numeric (integer and real) and Boolean

★ identify the two data structures required at National 5 level – variables and one-dimensional arrays

★ explain the use of constructs in SQA reference language:

  ★ expressions to assign values
  ★ expressions to return values using arithmetic operations (addition, subtraction, multiplication, division and exponentiation)
  ★ expressions to concatenate strings
  ★ selection constructs using simple conditional statements with <, >, ≤, ≥, =, ≠ operators
  ★ selection constructs using complex conditional statements
  ★ logical operators (AND, OR, NOT)
  ★ iteration and repetition using fixed and conditional loops
  ★ predefined functions (with parameters):

    ★ random
    ★ round
    ★ length

★ explain the use of standard algorithms in SQA reference language:

  ★ input validation
  ★ running total within loop
  ★ traversing a one-dimensional array.

SQA reference language

Examination questions that contain parts of programs will be written in SQA Reference Language. This is a language a lot like a programming language that you will have to be able to read, understand and explain. You do not have to write your answers or code in this language. This chapter contains examples of this language that you might see in National 5 question papers, together with the detail you are expected to give in your explanations that answer the questions. You will notice that the key words that make up commands are always in block capitals. Lower-case text is usually variable names or values to be used (such as text to be shown on screen).

Remember the five data types.

Data type	Description	Examples
Character	Any one punctuation symbol, letter or number that can be typed from the keyboard	A, z, &
String	A sequence of characters	Hello there, John, 08001111
Integer	A numeric data type, for whole numbers	35, 2017, 0
Real	A numeric data type, for numbers with a fractional part	0.2, 1.5, 3.14159265359
Boolean	True or false only	true, false

Input, output and assigning values

SQA Reference Language is often used to show part of a program, so sometimes variables will not be declared before they are used. To declare a string called "answer" with no initial value, you might see:

```
DECLARE answer AS STRING
```

To declare a Boolean called "complete" which is initially assigned to be false, you might see:

```
DECLARE complete AS BOOLEAN INITIALLY false
```

or to declare a real variable called "money" that is initially accepted from the keyboard, you might see:

```
DECLARE money AS REAL INITIALLY FROM KEYBOARD
```

If INITIALLY is used to set a value, you may not see the data type declared. Here is an array called trees, declared with a size of 4. Its data type is string:

```
DECLARE trees INITIALLY [ "Beech", "Oak",
"Pine", "Fir"]
```

The **FROM** keyword is often used for input and can come from other devices, for example, **FROM BARCODEREADER**. If the input from a device is happening after the variable has been declared, the **RECEIVE** keyword is also used. You *may* also see the data type expected in brackets before the name of the input device. So to get a name from the keyboard, you might see:

```
RECEIVE name FROM (STRING) KEYBOARD
```

If a variable is to be assigned a value that is not from an input device, the **SET** keyword is used. For example, to set a variable called 'wage' to 'hours_worked' multiplied by 'hourly_rate':

```
SET wage TO hours_worked * hourly_rate
```

If the intention was to show that wage on the screen along with an appropriate message, you might see:

```
SEND "The total wage is £" & wage TO DISPLAY
```

Output could also be sent **TO PRINTER**, or any other appropriate device.

The goal of SQA reference language is to be easily understood, so that you can answer questions about the effect of a whole list of instructions.

Assigning values may use any of the arithmetic operators:

Add	+
Subtract	–
Multiply	*
Divide	/
Power of	^

Questions

1 Fully explain the effect of each line of the following short part of a program:

```
Line 1   DECLARE price AS REAL INITIALLY 12.99
Line 2   RECEIVE order FROM (INTEGER) KEYBOARD
Line 3   SET total TO price * order
Line 4   SEND total TO DISPLAY
```

2 Fully explain the effect of each line of the following short part of a program:

```
Line 1   DECLARE initial AS CHAR
Line 2   SEND "Please enter your first initial" TO
         DISPLAY
Line 3   RECEIVE initial FROM (CHAR) KEYBOARD
```

Constructs

Conditional statements

Conditional statements are used to check some variable or input before deciding which instruction(s) to move on to next. An example might be if the player's score is higher than the high score, set it to be the high score:

```
IF player_score > highest_score THEN
  SET highest_score TO player_score
END IF
```

Multiple 'else if' parts are possible, as is an 'else' part. For example, to set a grade based on a pupil's percentage mark:

```
IF percent ≥ 70 THEN
  SET grade TO "A"
ELSE IF percent ≥ 60 THEN
  SET grade TO "B"
ELSE IF percent ≥ 50 THEN
  SET grade to "C"
ELSE IF percent ≥ 40 THEN
  SET grade to "D"
ELSE
  SET grade to "F"
END IF
```

Key points

Conditional statements (*If*)

A conditional statement is a way of making a choice in a programming language. A simple *If* statement allows you to choose to do or not to do an action. Groups of actions can be contained in *If* statements and, by using *If … then … else*, you can choose one 'branch' over another. The code in the following table gives examples of each of these uses of *If*.

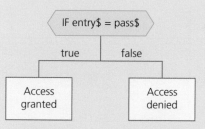

Scratch	Visual Basic

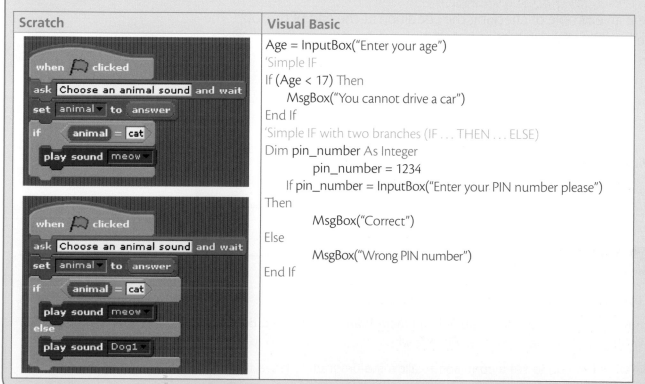	Age = InputBox("Enter your age")
	'Simple IF
	If (Age < 17) Then
	    MsgBox("You cannot drive a car")
	End If
	'Simple IF with two branches (IF … THEN … ELSE)
	Dim pin_number As Integer
	    pin_number = 1234
	  If pin_number = InputBox("Enter your PIN number please")
	Then
	    MsgBox("Correct")
	Else
	    MsgBox("Wrong PIN number")
	End If

3 Fully explain the effect of each line in the part of a program shown:

```
Line 1   RECEIVE player_rating FROM (INTEGER) KEYBOARD
Line 2   IF player_rating < 65 THEN
Line 3         SET category TO "Bronze"
Line 4   ELSE  IF player_rating <75 THEN
Line 5         SET category TO "Silver"
Line 6   ELSE
Line 7         SET category TO "Gold"
```

4 What command would you expect to see as Line 8?

Conditional loops

Conditional loops are loops that execute while, or until, a certain condition is true. The logical **condition** can be checked at the beginning of the loop (in which case the loop may not be executed at all) or the end of the loop. Here is an example of checking the condition at the start of the loop. The code is repeated while the user has not answered correctly and has not had three tries at answering:

```
    WHILE tries < 3 AND user_answer ≠ correct_answer
      SEND question TO DISPLAY
      RECEIVE user_answer FROM KEYBOARD
      SET tries TO tries  +  1
    END WHILE
```

Here is an example of checking the condition at the end of the loop. The code is repeated until the total of all the numbers entered by the user is more than 100:

```
    REPEAT
      SEND "Enter a number please" TO DISPLAY
      RECEIVE number FROM KEYBOARD
      SET total TO total  +  number
    UNTIL total > 100
```

Key points !

Conditional loops

It may be that you want to do something more than once, but you don't know how often you will need to do it. Here is where the conditional loop comes in.

This will allow you to set a condition to allow the program to leave the loop.

Scratch	Visual Basic

repeat until Y axis > 100
 glide **1** secs to x: X axis y: Y axis
 change X axis ▾ by **6**
 change Y axis ▾ by **6**
 change movements ▾ by **1**
	Do
	   Password = InputBox("Enter password")
	Loop Until Password = "fruitbat"
	Do
	   cost= InputBox("Enter cost")
	   total = total + cost
	Loop Until total > 200
	password = InputBox("Please enter your password")
	  Do While password < > 0
	  "fruitbat"
	    Password =
	    InputBox("Wrong password, please re-enter")
	Loop

Question ?

5 Fully explain the effect of each line in the part of a program shown:

```
Line 1   REPEAT
Line 2        SEND "How many bits are in one byte?"
              TO DISPLAY
Line 3        RECEIVE number FROM KEYBOARD
Line 4   UNTIL number=8
```

Conditional loops and conditional statements both involve the use of logical operators:

Greater than	>
Less than	<
Equals	=
Greater than or equal to	≥
Less than or equal to	≤
Does not equal	≠

Key points !

Complex conditions and the logical operators

The *If* statements and conditional loops contained simple conditions that were based on one thing being true or false. Complex conditions can depend on two or more things.

These conditions can be combined using the logical operators *AND*, *OR* and *NOT*.

* For the whole *AND* condition to be *true*, both parts have to be *true*.
* For the whole *OR* condition to be *true*, *either* part can be *true*.
* For the *NOT* to be *true*, the condition it applies to must be *false*.

To give an example of the difference between each of these, see the diagrams below. The shaded area in diagram A represents those pupils in a class who are *female AND* have *blue* eyes (the blue-eyed females only). The shaded area in diagram O represents those pupils in the class who are *female OR* have *blue* eyes (every female plus the blue-eyed boys). Diagram N shows those pupils who have *blue* eyes *AND* who are *NOT female*.

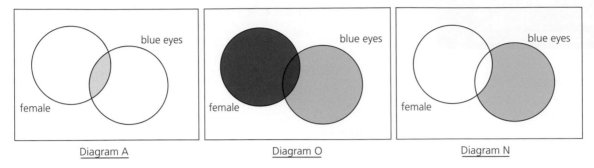

| Diagram A | Diagram O | Diagram N |

The following examples of code illustrate the use of AND, OR and NOT.

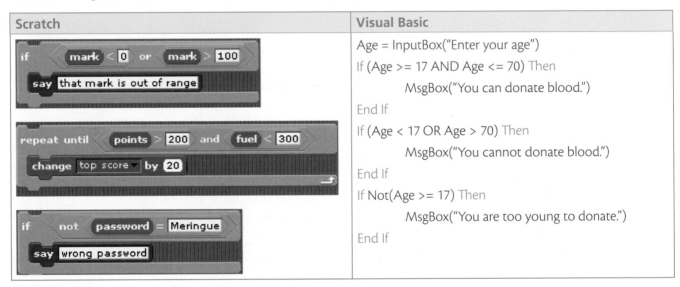

Scratch	Visual Basic

Visual Basic:
```
Age = InputBox("Enter your age")
If (Age >= 17 AND Age <= 70) Then
        MsgBox("You can donate blood.")
End If
If (Age < 17 OR Age > 70) Then
        MsgBox("You cannot donate blood.")
End If
If Not(Age >= 17) Then
        MsgBox("You are too young to donate.")
End If
```

Fixed loops

Fixed loops are loops that repeat a set number of times. SQA Reference Language allows the integer variable that controls the loop to be visible within the code, as you often did in Visual Basic. An example of this would be using the counter variable to control a fixed loop of five times, by beginning the fixed loop with the line:

```
FOR counter FROM 0 TO 4 DO
```

This fixed loop will end with **END FOR**.

However, you may also see a fixed loop where the set number doesn't appear, instead it is to loop for all of the items in an array. There are a number of ways this might be shown. If there was an array called 'scores' you might see:

```
        FOR counter FROM 0 TO <End Of List> DO
```

or

```
        FOR EACH score FROM scores DO
```

Fixed loops

When you have a piece of code that you want the computer to repeat a set number of times, you would use a fixed loop as shown in the screenshot in the table:

Scratch	Visual Basic

	'Fixed Loop example
	For counter = 1 to 5
	    name = Inputbox("Enter the name of a pupil in your class please")
	    Msgbox("The name you entered was" & name)
	Next

Questions ?

6 Fully explain the effect of each line in the part of a program below:

```
Line 1   RECEIVE multiple FROM (REAL) KEYBOARD
Line 2   FOR times = 1 TO 10 DO
Line 3       SET answer TO multiple * times
Line 4       SEND multiple & " × " & times & " = "
             & answer TO DISPLAY
Line 5   END FOR
```

7 Show exactly what the output to the screen would be from the above code if at Line 1 the entry at the keyboard was '2'.

Standard algorithms

An algorithm is a plan or list of steps to solve a problem. Some problems that occur regularly in programming now have a set list of steps to solve that problem. This is known as a **standard algorithm**. There are three standard algorithms in the National 5 course.

Traversing a one-dimensional array

Simply put, **traversing** a one-dimensional array just means accessing all the values in the array. It might be to set the values based on input, to check the values against a condition, or to output the values on the screen.

In programming, in order to get a value from an array you have to index the array. This means using an integer (often in brackets) to indicate which element from the array that you wish to use.

Here is the SQA Reference Language to traverse a one-dimensional array using the loop variable 'counter' to index the array. The array is a list of names that will be shown on the screen:

```
FOR counter FROM 0 TO <End Of List> DO
     SEND names(counter) TO DISPLAY
END FOR
```

However, you might also see an array traversed using a fixed loop where the loop variable is not stated, so the **indexing** of the array doesn't appear to take place in what you read:

```
FOR EACH entry FROM names DO
     SEND entry TO DISPLAY
END FOR
```

You can see an example of this in Scratch in Chapter 2, page 25 and in Visual Basic in 'Setting up and filling an array', Chapter 3, page 66.

Running total within a loop

This means to keep track of a total while your program repeats instructions (using either a fixed loop or a conditional loop) that may or may not involve updating the total. There are many different situations where this may apply. Uses of this algorithm may or may not involve input from the user, and they may or may not involve a conditional statement. The example below uses both:

The following SQA Reference Language will ask ten users to enter their age, and keep a total of how many are eligible to donate blood. It uses a fixed loop.

```
DECLARE total AS INTEGER INITIALLY 0
FOR counter FROM 0 TO 9 DO
     SEND "Enter age" TO DISPLAY
     RECEIVE age FROM DISPLAY
     IF age >=17 AND age <= 70 THEN
          SET total TO total  +  1
     END IF
END FOR
SEND total & " out of 10 people can donate blood"
TO DISPLAY
```

You can see an example of this in Scratch in Chapter 2, page 21 and in Visual Basic in Chapter 3, page 57.

Input validation

Input validation is including code in your program so that the data that is entered is repeatedly checked to ensure that it is sensible. If the data entered as an input is not within the acceptable limits, the user should be shown a useful message to help them understand why the input wasn't accepted. The program should then allow the user to re-enter the data. However, the program should continue to check the data that has been input until the entry is acceptable, that is, data that is valid.

Example

The following SQA Reference Language will ask for a character that is 'y' or 'n'.

```
REPEAT
     SEND "Enter choice (y/n)" TO DISPLAY
     RECEIVE selection FROM KEYBOARD
     IF selection ≠ "y" AND selection ≠ "n" THEN
          SEND "Invalid entry, please enter y or n" TO DISPLAY
     END IF
UNTIL selection = "y" OR selection = "n"
```

You can see an example of this in Visual Basic in Chapter 3, page 58.

Predefined functions

A **predefined function** is included with the programming language, it does not have to be coded by the programmer. When a predefined function is called, it needs some data sent in – known as **parameters**. The parameters are put inside brackets. A predefined function always returns one value to be used by the program.

SQA Reference Language currently has no rules for how predefined functions will be shown.

Round

Round accepts two parameters, the first being the number to be rounded, the second being the number of decimal places to round it to.

Example

The following example is how SQA Reference Language is likely to round a variable called 'average_income' to two decimal places and put the result in a variable called 'final_income':

```
SET final_income TO ROUND (average_income, 2)
```

You can see an example of this in Visual Basic in Chapter 3, page 68.

Length

Length accepts one parameter, a string. It returns an integer of the number of characters in the string.

Example

The following example is how SQA Reference Language is likely to find the length of a string variable called 'car_registration' and put the result in a variable called 'reg_length':

```
SET reg_length TO LENGTH(car_registration)
```

You can see an example of this in Visual Basic in Chapter 3, Activity 37, page 70.

Random

Random is used to get a random number. However, in most programming languages it needs no parameters, returns a random number between 0 and 1, and then arithmetic is used to convert this into a random number of the kind the programmer is looking for.

You can see an example of this in Visual Basic in Chapter 3, page 69.

String concatenation

String concatenation is used to join two or more strings together to make a new string.

Example

In SQA Reference Language this uses the '&' symbol:

```
SET full_name TO forename & " " & surname
```

You can see an example of this in Visual Basic in Chapter 3, page 71.

Chapter 5

Testing, documentation and evaluation (software)

The testing stage

Once the code has been entered, and all the typing mistakes removed, it has to be tested with a range of inputs to make sure that it does the job it is meant to do and that it does not keep crashing all the time. The three types of data that have to be tested are normal, extreme and exceptional. These are also called 'in range', 'boundary' and 'out of range'. Below is a table of test data used to test a subprogram which validates data input as whole percentages.

Test data	Type of testing	Expected accept/ reject	Actual accept/ reject
6	Normal	accept	
21	Normal	accept	
57	Normal	accept	
99	Normal	accept	
0	Extreme	accept	
100	Extreme	accept	
−1	Exceptional	reject	
101	Exceptional	reject	
69.2	Exceptional	reject	

When selecting test data to be used, the programmers go back to the statement about the problem that was agreed at the analysis stage (the software specification) to help them choose suitable data to be input.

Where a program contains a condition (e.g. if percentage >=50) then test data on that boundary is also considered to be Extreme (i.e. 50 would be extreme test data for that program).

Types of error

Syntax error

This is an error resulting from breaking the rules of the language, for example:

```
IF total > 100 THEN
PRINT "You have exceeded the maximum"
END
```

The missing *end If* (line 3) will produce an error message.

Syntax errors are found by the translator program (interpreter or compiler, more on these in Chapter 7).

Execution error

This is an error that occurs while the program is running. It can happen if you try to access an array element beyond the size of the array, or try to divide by zero. Testing with exceptional data can help to find some **execution errors**, but will not ensure that there will definitely be no execution errors.

Logic error

This is an error that produces incorrect results but does not stop the program from running. It is caused by an error in the design of the program, such as a badly written complex condition:

```
IF total < 1 OR total > 99 THEN
```

This fails to correctly check a range of between 0 and 100.

Logic errors are found by testing.

1 How can a programmer be sure to select good test data?
2 A program has been developed that involves the input of someone's height as a real number of metres between 0.01 and 350. Identify one item of data for each of 'normal', 'extreme' and 'exceptional' test data for this input.
3 What kind of error is shown here?

```
IF password = "entry4126" THEN
   PRUNT "Password accepted"
END IF
```

4 Dan's program crashed when it asked for a number between 1 and 5 and the user entered 7.
   a) What kind of error has occurred?
   b) What kind of test data should have been used to find this error at the testing stage?
   c) Which standard algorithm could be used in the code to prevent this error occurring?

The documentation stage

Two pieces of documentation are commonly produced at the **documentation stage:** the **user guide** and the technical guide.

User guide

This explains how to use the software. It may contain a manual, a tutorial and/or troubleshooting tips. It will tell the user how to give commands to the program, for example, what keys to press or how to make choices.

Technical guide

This will explain the system requirements needed to run the software. It will say what operating system is needed, how much RAM is required, the **processor** clock speed and number of cores needed and how much storage space is required. The **technical guide** also explains how to install the program.

The evaluation stage

The **evaluation stage** is when programmers look at the solution that they have created and consider how good their program is. At National 5 level this is evaluated under four headings: fitness for purpose, efficient use of coding constructs, robustness and readability.

Fitness for purpose

Programmers go back to the statement about the problem that was agreed at the analysis stage (the software specification) and compare this with the results of the testing stage.

If the program has been successfully proven to meet all of the points given in the problem or detailed in the statement about the problem that was agreed at the analysis stage (the software specification), then it can be said to be fit for purpose.

If you are writing an evaluation of **fitness for purpose**, be sure to mention:
- each individual thing that the program was required to do
- that it does each of those things
- how you know that it does each of them (refer to your testing).

Efficient use of coding constructs

The programmers look at their code and identify any places where they have used more code than was actually needed to solve the problem. In practice, **efficient code** will ensure there is no unnecessary use of the **central processing unit** (CPU) or RAM.

> ## Example ⚑
>
> Lilla owns an ice-cream van business. There are four ice-cream vans each with a different driver. Lilla wants a program to ask each driver how much money they made that day, and show the total money made for the company.
>
>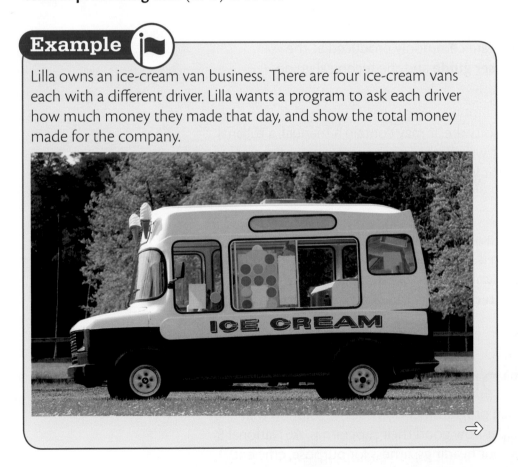
>
> ⇨

Inefficient solution:

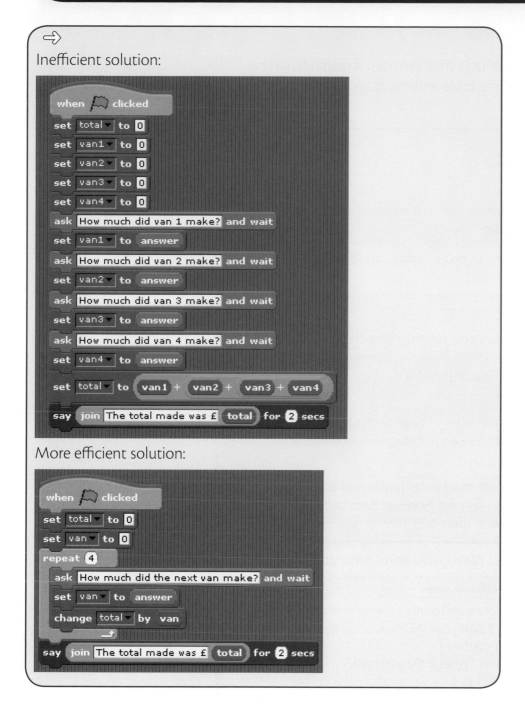

More efficient solution:

So if evaluating the efficient use of coding constructs for the first solution, you might say:

The solution involves repeated sections of similar code. This part could have been coded more efficiently if a fixed loop had been used. This would have saved the programmer time.

Robustness

A robust program is one that does not crash easily. Robust programs will have input validation so that they don't crash due to invalid input. Your testing that involved entering exceptional test data can be used to prove that your program is robust. If your program experiences execution errors, then it is not robust.

Readability

Programmers should make sure that their program is readable, so that other people can understand the code and maintain it if necessary.

The table below gives examples of readable and unreadable code.

Poor code	Readable code

let x = 0
print "pass mark";
input a
for p = 1 to 20
print "mark";
input m
if m >= p then let x = x + 1
next p
print x;"passed"
end
	! A program to count the number of passes
	! in a class of 20. All marks are percentages.
	LET count = 0
	PRINT "What is the pass mark";
	INPUT pass
	FOR pupil = 1 TO 20
	    PRINT "What is the mark for pupil"; pupil; "?"
	    INPUT mark
	    IF mark >= pass THEN
	      LET count = count + 1
	    END IF
	NEXT pupil
	PRINT "A total of"; count; "pupils passed the test."
	END

Questions

5 Chiara is considering her program's fitness for purpose at the evaluation stage. Which other two stages of the development process will help her in doing this?

6 Which kind of error occurs in programs that are not robust?

7 Why is it desirable to have readable code?

Section 2 Computer Systems

Chapter 6

Data representation

What you should know

By the end of this chapter you should **know** and **understand**:

★ how to describe and exemplify the use of binary to represent positive integers, including conversion from binary to denary and vice-versa

★ how to describe floating point representation of positive real numbers using the terms mantissa and exponent

★ that extended ASCII code (8-bit) is used to represent characters

★ how to describe the vector graphics method of graphic representation for the common objects of rectangle, ellipse, line and polygon each with attributes including co-ordinates, fill colour and line colour

★ how to describe the bit-mapped method of graphics representation.

Binary and denary numbers

Binary is the number system that has only two digits, those being 0 and 1. **Denary** (sometimes called decimal) is the number system that you are used to that has 10 digits, those being 0, 1, 2, 3, 4, 5, 6, 7, 8, and 9.

Using binary to represent positive integers

Computers use binary numbers. To work with denary numbers, the computer has to convert them to binary. The table below will help you understand how to convert them.

2^7	2^6	2^5	2^4	2^3	2^2	2^1	2^0	Power of 2
128	64	32	16	8	4	2	1	Denary equivalent

The denary number 66 is stored as 01000010 in binary.

2^7	2^6	2^5	2^4	2^3	2^2	2^1	2^0	Power of 2
128	64	32	16	8	4	2	1	Denary equivalent
0	1	0	0	0	0	1	0	= 64 + 2 = 66

Example

Convert the number 10011100 into denary.

Step 1: Write down the place values for the eight binary digits. You start with '1' as the right-most place value, and double each time as you move left one place, until you've written eight place values. The highest place value should end up as 128 (in National 5 you will never have to convert an integer of larger than eight bits).

128	64	32	16	8	4	2	1

Step 2: Write the binary number so that each digit lines up under its corresponding place value.

128	64	32	16	8	4	2	1
1	0	0	1	1	1	0	0

Step 3: Where there is a 1, add up all those place values.

128 + 16 + 8 + 4 = 156

The answer is 156.

Example

Convert the number 92 into binary.

Step 1: Write down the place values for the eight binary digits, just like Step 1 of the previous example.

128	64	32	16	8	4	2	1

Step 2: Starting at the left, the highest place value, if the number you have is equal to or higher than that, write a 1, and take the place value away from the number you have left. If it is not, write a 0.

128	64	32	16	8	4	2	1
0							

Denary number left is 92.

Step 3: Repeat Step 2 for the next place value.

128	64	32	16	8	4	2	1
0	1						

Denary number left is 92 − 64 = 28.

Keep repeating Step 2 for each place value until you have 0 left.

128	64	32	16	8	4	2	1
0	1	0					

Denary number left is 28.

128	64	32	16	8	4	2	1
0	1	0	1				

Denary number left is 28 − 16 = 12.

128	64	32	16	8	4	2	1
0	1	0	1	1			

Denary number left is 12 − 8 = 4.

⇒

128	64	32	16	8	4	2	1
0	1	0	1	1	1		

Denary number left is 4 – 4 = 0.

We have nothing left so the rest of the digits are zero.

128	64	32	16	8	4	2	1
0	1	0	1	1	1	0	0

So denary 92 is 01011100 in binary.

Questions

1 What is an integer?
2 Convert 01100111 into denary.
3 Convert 184 into binary.

Using binary to represent real numbers

In subjects like physics and maths, you may learn about scientific notation, also known as 'standard form'. This is a way of writing numbers that are very large or very small numbers containing a decimal point. In fact, computers store all real numbers using this format. We call this '**floating point representation**'.

545 000 000 is a very large number. This would instead be written as 5.45×10^8. The small number, 8, is the exponent. That is because the decimal point has had to move eight places to the left for us to go to 5.45 from 545 000 000. In this example, 5.45 is the mantissa.

If we were writing 0.000926 in this way, it would be written as 9.26×10^{-4}. Here the exponent is −4. This is because the decimal point has had to move four places to the right for us to go to 9.26 from 0.000926. In this example, 9.26 is the mantissa.

You will not have to convert real numbers between binary and denary, you only have to know that the computer stores a mantissa in binary and an exponent in binary. In fact, binary is a number system based on two digits, so a binary number in this notation would actually look like this:

Key points !

Representing real numbers

Real numbers are represented using floating point.

In floating point, numbers are divided into base/mantissa/exponent.

Any number that is a power of 10 can be represented with a decimal point in a fixed position, so $137.598 = 1.37598 \times 10^2$.

Decimal example

Mantissa	Exponent	Base
1.37598	2	10

In binary, you might want to store 1101110000 using floating point notation:

Binary example

Mantissa	Exponent	Base
110111	100	2

Storing text
Extended ASCII

Text is represented using **extended ASCII** code. **ASCII** stands for American Standard Code for Information Interchange.

Extended ASCII is an 8-bit code which provides 256 code values. This gives us 32 control characters (non-printable characters like the keys 'Escape' or 'Backspace') and 224 regular characters.

Each of the characters in the **character set** has a unique value. The character set is the range of characters available to the user.

This includes:
- non-printing control characters such as <return> or <tab>
- upper- and lower-case letters such as A–Z, a–z
- numbers such as 0–9
- punctuation and other symbols such as $ & * ^ @ ":
- some commonly used letters from other languages like ö or é.

An extract of the binary code is shown below:

Extended ASCII	Denary equivalent	Representing character
01000001	65	A
01000010	66	B
01000011	67	C
01000100	68	D
01000101	69	E
01000110	70	F

Questions ?

4 The binary number 0.0010101 is being stored as 10101×2^{-111}. Identify which number is the mantissa and which is the exponent.
5 What is meant by the term 'control character'?
6 What is meant by the term 'character set'?
7 How many bits are needed to store the word 'hello' using extended ASCII?
8 How many different possible characters are there in extended ASCII?

Storing graphics
Vector storage

In a vector, or object-oriented, graphic the image is made up of a number of shapes layered on top of one another to make up the picture.

Each object in the picture is described mathematically as a list of **attributes**. These fully describe the *type* of object, its start *position* on

screen using *x* and *y* co-ordinates, its *size* and the *colour/pattern* of its outline (called *line*) and middle (called *fill*). Other attributes might be the degree of any *rotation* and which *layer* it is on.

These instructions, which describe the **vector graphic**, are then translated into bitmaps and binary numbers before the graphic can be displayed on the screen. Vector graphics are coded by developers using a language called SVG (scalable vector graphics).

Key points !

SVG Code

This section covers the SVG code for rectangle, ellipse, line and polygon objects, along with attributes *x* co-ordinate, *y* co-ordinate, fill colour and line colour. SVG code is often included within the **HTML** code of a web page.

An SVG area will begin with a tag like this:

```
<svg width="400" height="300">
```

This tells the **browser** to use an area of 400×300 **pixels** to draw the shapes in. The instructions for the shapes will follow, then the SVG section of the web page code will end with `</svg>`.

Rectangle SVG example

```
<rect x="10" y="20" width="150" height="100"
    style="fill:blue;stroke:black;stroke-width:3" />
```

will show a rectangle beginning at co-ordinates (10,20) that is 150 pixels wide and 100 pixels high. It will be blue with a black outline and the outline will be three pixels wide.

Ellipse SVG example

An ellipse can be used to draw a circle or an oval. The attributes 'rx' and 'ry' represent the length of the *radius*. The radius is the distance from the centre to the edge (the outline).

```
<ellipse cx="120" cy="100" rx="40" ry="25" style
="fill:red;stroke:blue;stroke-width:5" />
```

will show an oval with the centre at co-ordinates (120,100) that has a radius to the right and left that is 40 pixels (so 80 pixels wide in total) and has radius to the top and bottom that is 25 pixels (so it is 50 pixels high in total). It will be red with a blue outline and the outline will be five pixels wide.

Line SVG example

```
<line x1="20" y1="18" x2="150" y2="170"
style="stroke:purple;stroke-width:2" />
```

will show a line beginning at co-ordinates (20,18) and ending at co-ordinates (150,170). It will be purple and two pixels wide.

⇒

Polygon SVG example

'Poly' means many. A polygon is a shape with shape many sides. That means the polygon SVG object can be used to draw a triangle, a square, a pentagon, a hexagon, and so on … but also a many-sided shape that is not a regular shape, because the sides and angles are not equal, like this:

```
<polygon points="140,10 160,15 190,60 165,
100 120,80" style="fill:blue;stroke:black;
stroke-width:3" />
```

will show a five-sided shape (because there are five pairs of co-ordinates) beginning at co-ordinates (140,10). The outline will then go to (160,15) then to (190,60) then to (165,100) then to (120,80) before ending back where it started at (140,10). It will be blue with a black outline and the outline will be 3 pixels wide:

Bit-mapped storage

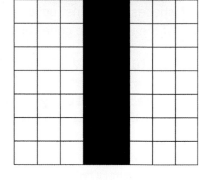

Bit-mapped graphics are made up of **pixels**. Look at the diagram on the right.

If the image is black and white, each pixel is represented by patterns of binary numbers where each square or pixel filled in = 1, and each square or pixel left blank = 0.

However, if the graphic is in colour, instead of 1 bit for each pixel, there will be a colour code. This will involve a number of bits per pixel. The number of bits per pixel is called the bit depth (or sometimes **colour depth**).

If the bit depth was 3 bits, there would be 2^3 possible colour codes: 000, 001, 010, 011, 100, 101, 110, 111. 2^3 = eight possible colours if the bit depth is 3 bits.

However, most digital devices use a bit depth of 24 bits, which is over sixteen million possible colours!

Key point

Resolution and calculating file size

The number of pixels that make up the screen or image is known as the '**resolution**'. This is often seen in the format 800×600, or similar. You might also see this as a number of megapixels (million pixels) or in dpi (**dots per inch**).

If the resolution is in dpi, you have to work out the number of pixels:
* resolution = length (in inches) × dpi × breadth (in inches) × dpi.

The file size of an uncompressed bit-mapped graphic can be calculated using the formula:
* file size (in bits) = resolution × bit depth (in bits).

Comparing vector and bit-mapped graphics

- Bitmaps tend to take up more space than vector graphics, as vector graphics are stored as text.
- Bitmap packages lose the underlying pixel data when shapes overlap. Vector graphics store the shapes separately so overlapping has no loss of data.
- Bitmap images are created at a set number of pixels so a set resolution. Vector graphics are used as instructions by the computer to draw the shapes so vector graphics can be scaled up with no loss of quality. This is called **resolution independence**.
- Bitmaps enable you to edit individual pixels. A vector graphic will allow you to change only attributes of an entire object, for example, fill colour, line colour, line thickness.
- Vector graphics require distinct shapes and so are not suitable for photographs. Captured images will be saved as bitmaps.

Hints & tips

Units of memory/ storage capacity

*8 bits = 1 **byte***
*1024 bytes = 1 **kibibyte***
*1024 KiB = 1 **mebibyte***
*1024 MiB = 1 **gibibyte***
*1024 GiB = 1 **tebibyte***
(TiB)

Questions ?

9 Which method of storing images allows shapes to be layered?
10 Which method of storing images must be used for captured photographs?
11 Which method of storing images has resolution independence?
12 Which method of storing images allows editing of individual pixels?

Computer structure

What you should know

By the end of this chapter you should **know** and **understand**:

★ how to describe the purpose of the basic computer architecture components and how they are linked together:
  * **processor** (registers, ALU, control unit)
  * memory locations with unique addresses
  * buses (data and address)
★ the need for interpreters and compilers to translate high-level program code to binary (machine code instructions).

Key points

Computer systems

* have at their core a processor which acts as the 'brains' of the computer
* store data in memory
* use buses to move data around, for example, to transfer data to and from the memory
* use interfaces to communicate with external devices such as printers, monitors, cameras, games controllers, etc.

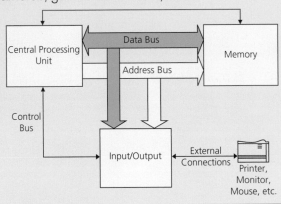

The processor

The processor is at the centre of all of the computer's operations and deals with all the movement of data and any calculations to be carried out. A processor is a number of layers of silicon crystal wafers on which millions of tiny electronic components are etched. It is made up of three important components: the control unit (CU), the arithmetic and logic unit (ALU) and registers.

Arithmetic and logic unit (ALU)

The **arithmetic and logic unit** (ALU) is the part of the processor that performs all the calculations (like **LET total=cost*quantity**). This part also makes all the logical decisions (like **IF age>17 THEN**).

Control unit

This is the part of the processor that performs a number of functions. One function of the **control unit** is to decode and execute the instructions. Another is to keep all the components in time with one another using the clock line. The control unit also initiates memory accesses using the read line or write line.

Registers

Registers are storage locations that are internal to the processor. They are used to:

- store data that is being transferred to or from memory
- hold the address of the location in memory which the processor is accessing to read or write data
- hold the instructions that are being carried out.

Computer memory

Main memory can be either random access memory (**RAM**) or read only memory (**ROM**). RAM is the working space of the computer. It holds all of the programs and data files currently in use by the system and users. ROM is system memory which holds vital systems information, for example, start-up instructions.

RAM

- The processor can write to, or read from, RAM at high speed.
- Data held in RAM *can* be changed.
- All data in RAM is *lost* when the power is switched off.
- RAM holds all the data and programs currently in use.
- Each **memory location** in RAM has its own unique address.

ROM

- Data is stored permanently in ROM – it is not lost when the power is switched off.
- Data in ROM *cannot* be changed.
- ROM holds vital systems data and programs.

Buses

Buses are used as transmitters between the different parts of a computer system. The two main buses are the **data bus** and the **address bus**.

The data bus

The lines on the data bus provide a path for data to be transferred between system modules, for example, between main memory and the processor.

The number of lines of data = the width of the bus. Each line can carry one bit, therefore a 32-bit data bus can transfer 32 bits at a time. The width of the data bus is important when determining how efficiently a system performs.

The address bus

The address bus transfers the address of the memory location where data is about to be stored or from which data is about to be read. In theory, the more lines on the address bus, the more locations the system can address. This bus only operates in one direction: carrying addresses from the processor to main memory.

Machine code

Machine code is the language that the computer understands at the lowest level. In machine code, the instructions are made up of binary numbers and look like the box on the right.

The disadvantage is that they are very difficult to read and understand. Programs written in high level languages like Visual Basic need to be translated into machine code.

```
01101101
11001100
01011100
11110000
```

Translators

Remember, at the lowest level, the system only understands machine code. All programs written in a **high-level language** need to be translated into machine code before the instructions can be carried out by the system. We use translator programs to carry out this translation. An example of this is shown below.

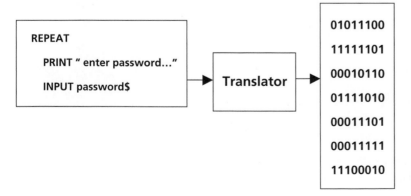

There are two different types of translator, each with its own advantages and disadvantages. They are compilers and interpreters.

Interpreter

An **interpreter** does not produce object code. Object code is a saved translated version of the program, in machine code. The translator translates and executes each line of the program in turn every time the program is run.

Advantages of using an interpreter

- If errors are present, then they are highlighted immediately and are therefore easier to detect and fix.
- Interpreters can run partial code or code under development.

Disadvantages of using an interpreter

- As translation is not saved, the interpreter must be present to run code.
- If code is repeated, as in a loop, the code is translated and run many times.
- Individual runs are slower, due to the above two points.

Compiler

A **compiler** translates high-level language instructions, called source code, into machine code, object code. It does this by going through the source one line at a time and translating it. It puts the translation in a file and moves on. When the whole program is translated, the object code can be run. There is no need to translate the source again, unless the program is changed. If there are any syntax errors – errors in grammar – it lists them. The object code cannot be run until the whole program is translated.

Advantages of a compiler

- If no errors are found, then the source does not need to be translated again.
- The translator program is no longer required once the program is translated.

Disadvantages of a compiler

- If any syntax errors are present then the program will not run.
- The errors may be harder to correct, as problems may not be identified until the code is translated.

Questions

1 An instruction is being fetched from main memory and sent to the processor.
   a) Which bus will transfer the instruction from memory to the processor?
   b) Where will the instruction be stored once it arrives at the processor?
2 What is the job of the ALU?
3 How does the computer distinguish between the memory locations in RAM?
4 What are machine code instructions made up of?
5 Which translator program translates code line by line?
6 Which translator program saves the machine code version of the program after translation occurs?

What you should know

By the end of this chapter you should **know** and **understand**:

★ the role of **firewalls** in protecting computer security
★ the use made of encryption in electronic communications
★ how to describe the energy use of computer systems, the implications for the environment and how these could be reduced through:

  ★ settings on monitors
  ★ power-down settings
  ★ leaving computers on standby.

Security precautions

Firewall

A firewall provides a means of checking all data coming into and going out of a network. The firewall decides which packets of data are allowed through to their destination address. A firewall can be software running on:

- an individual machine (you should have one on your home computer)
- servers across a network (these are called distributed firewalls).

Firewalls are often built into an operating system or are provided by the security suite. On a large-scale network, the firewall software often runs on a dedicated computer.

A firewall may also be implemented in hardware, or as a combination of hardware and software.

Key points

The purpose of the firewall is to prevent **hacking**. Hacking is gaining access to data without permission.

However, a firewall is not designed to protect against viruses.

It is best to have up-to-date antivirus software working on your system in addition to having a firewall.

Encryption

You can protect data by using **encryption**. This means putting the data into a code that a hacker can't understand without having the key to the code.

Encryption is especially important when transmitting sensitive data using a wireless network. This is because it is relatively easy to intercept. You should avoid using unsecure public wifi hotspots to send sensitive data.

Hints & tips

Websites that use encryption to protect your data in transit have 'https' at the beginning of the URL.

Questions

1 Explain two ways to prevent a hacker from accessing data.
2 What will someone see if they intercept encrypted data during transmission?

Environmental implications

Energy use

High energy use is bad for the environment because a high percentage of energy is generated using non-renewable fossil fuels. This involves further energy to mine and transport materials, with mines possibly scarring the landscape. The production of energy from fossil fuels causes the release of CO_2 into the atmosphere, contributing to air pollution and global warming via the greenhouse effect.

Computers use lots of energy. A typical desktop computer with a 17-inch LCD monitor requires 110 watts for the computer and 35 watts for the monitor, giving a total of 145 watts. However, while in standby mode it uses only 5–10 watts.

The servers that power the internet can use up vast amounts of energy. For example, HP's Redstone can incorporate up to 2800 servers in a rack.

This high level of energy also means high financial costs in terms of the electricity bill.

Key points !

Saving energy

Settings on monitors

The brightness level can be reduced to save energy. Also, the monitor can automatically switch off after a certain time period of user inactivity. A third of a computer's energy use is used by the monitor.

Power down settings

Computers can be set to shut down automatically at a certain time of day. This is especially useful in a workplace.

Leaving computers on standby

Standby mode will switch off the monitor and also stop the hard drive from spinning, saving energy. In some cases the processor is powered down, with the current state (for example, contents of registers) being put in main memory (RAM).

Did you know? ★

A computer monitor switched off for one night saves enough energy to microwave six meals.

Questions

3 Why is high energy use bad for the environment?

4 How does standby mode save energy?

What you should know

By the end of this chapter you should **know** and **understand**:

★ how to identify the end-user and functional requirements of a database problem

★ how to create entity-relationship diagrams with two entities indicating entity name, attributes and relationship (one to many)

★ how to create a **data dictionary** including entity name, attribute name, primary or foreign key, attribute type, attribute size and validation

★ the five attribute types: text, number, date, time, Boolean

★ the four kinds of database validation: presence check, restricted choice, field length and **range**

★ how to design a query including multiple tables and fields, the search criteria and the sort order

★ the implications for individuals and businesses of the Data Protection Act 1998.

Analysing a database problem

Functional requirements

Functional requirements are to fulfil the reason that the database is to be created. These will include the data that has to be stored and queries that have to be able to be performed.

End-user requirements

End-user requirements are facilities or features that have to be included to ensure that users are able to access and carry out the functions included in the database.

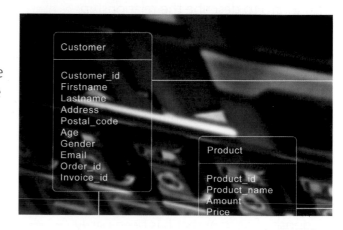

Example

Papa Steel is a company that sells high quality metals. They have offices in Kilmarnock and Nice. A database is required to store details of all the metal products, and also details of the orders from customers. The database users may speak English or French so the interface must be available in both languages. The users must be able to search details of products or orders, or sort data on those details. Some users have poor eyesight and require the facility to adjust what is seen on screen.

For the above example, functional requirements are:

- store fields and records about products in a table
- store fields and records about orders in a table
- search the products table
- search the order table
- sort the products table
- sort the order table.

End-user requirements are the ability to:

- select English or French language
- zoom/change font size
- access the search and sort functions.

Database design

Entity-relationship diagram

The **entity-relationship diagram** shows the entities of the database and the relationships between the entities. Each **entity** in the design will become a table in the implementation of the database. At National 5 level you will only ever have to show two entities, and the relationship will always be one to many. The entity that contains the **foreign key** is always on the 'many' side of the relationship. The relationship must be labelled with a verb to describe the relationship.

The entity-relationship diagram must also show the **attributes** of each entity. These will be the fields in each table. The attribute that is the **primary key** for each entity should be underlined. Any attribute which is a foreign key should have an asterisk (*) at the end of the attribute name.

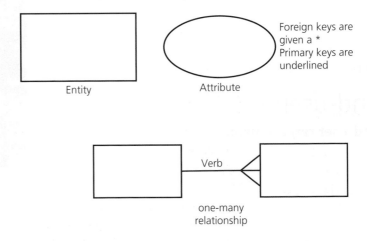

It is likely that in the examination paper you will only have to complete an entity-relationship diagram that has been partly done for you. However, in the assignment you may have to create a whole new entity-relationship diagram.

Example

The example of players playing for a sports team shows a one-to-many relationship. The 'many' side of a relationship is indicated by the 'crow's feet'.

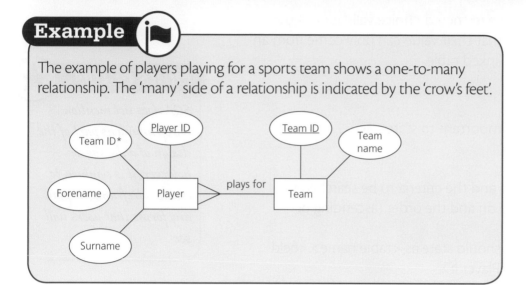

Attributes and validation

The attributes will each have a certain data type and are likely to also have **validation** rules that must be kept when data is entered into that field.

Attributes

Data type	Description	Example
Text	Any characters that can be typed from the keyboard.	aZ@%59
Number	A real number or an integer.	5.67
Date	A calendar date. The format can be customised.	12th November 2001
Time	A time. The format can be customised.	23:59
Boolean	True or False, often represented by a checkbox.	☑

Validation

Validation	Description	Example
Presence check	The field must have data entered for every record.	Cars must have a registration number. This can be done in MS Access by setting the 'Required' field property to 'Yes'.
Restricted choice	The data entered into the field must be selected from a list of **valid** possibilities.	Title could be restricted to Mr, Ms, Mrs, Miss. This can be done in MS Access by using the Lookup Wizard under the Data Type dropdown selection.
Field length	The data entered into the field must meet certain requirements on the number of characters.	Phone numbers must have 11 digits. This can be done in MS Access by setting the 'Validation Rule' field property to `"Len([Phone number])=11"`.
Range	The data entered into the field must meet certain limits.	Age must be 0 or more and less than or equal to 150. This can be done in MS Access by setting the 'Validation Rule' field property to `">=0" AND <=150`.

Foreign keys should always have restricted-choice validation, if the software in use allows this, so that their value can only come from an existing primary key from the linked table.

Query design

When designing a **query** it is important to state:
- what tables will be used
- what fields will be shown
- what fields will be searched and the criteria to be searched for
- what fields are to be sorted on and the order (ascending or descending)
- when stating the field, you should state as <table name>.<field name>, for example, Player.Player ID.

Hints & tips

SQA does not mention wireframing as part of the design of a database; however, it is common to create wireframes to plan any forms that users will see

Questions

1 State two possible functional requirements of a database.
2 In an entity-relationship diagram, how would you show a
   a) primary key?
   b) foreign key?
3 How does the foreign key help to indicate what the correct relationship is between entities?
4 Which attribute data type might appear as a checkbox?
5 Explain what is meant by 'restricted-choice' validation.
6 An attribute called 'Height in metres' is to include validation so that the value entered must be between 0.01 and 3. What kind of validation would be used to do this?
7 What will a presence check do?

Data Protection Act 1998

The **Data Protection Act 1998** is designed to protect members of the public from having their personal data (data about them) misused. If the Act is breached, individuals are often entitled to financial compensation from the business or organisation that was storing their personal data. At National 5 level we focus on four particular aspects of this law.

Prior consent of the data subject

The data subject is the person that the data is about. They must have given permission for the data to be stored for set purposes that they have been told about. This permission is often given through a signature on a document, but can also be given verbally on a telephone call or via an online **form**.

Data Protection
Act 1998

CHAPTER 29

First Published 1998
Reprinted Incorporating Corrections 2003

Data used for limited, specifically stated purposes

When the data subject gives permission for their data to be stored and used, the purposes for which it will be used must be stated. If the data is then used for any purpose outside of these specifically stated purposes, then the organisation doing so has broken the law. This also means that the organisation can only keep the data for a limited amount of time.

Accuracy of data

The organisation storing and using the personal data about the data subject must make sure that the data is accurate. This includes keeping data up to date as the subject's circumstances change.

Data kept safe and secure

If a hacker successfully gains access to personal data, the hacker has broken the Computer Misuse Act 1990, but the organisation storing the data has broken the Data Protection Act 1998. Organisations that store personal data must ensure that they have appropriate security precautions in place to prevent any unauthorised access to the data.

General Data Protection Regulation (GDPR)

On 25 May 2018, the Data Protection Act 1998 will be replaced by the **General Data Protection Regulation**. From session 2018–19 onwards the National 5 course will feature this law in place of the Data Protection Act 1998. The full version of this new law can be found online at https://gdpr-info.eu/, however, it is likely that SQA will limit the content within the National 5 course to the areas that correspond with the existing protection given by the Data Protection Act 1998, as detailed above.

Implementation (database)

By the end of this chapter you should **know** and **understand**:

★ how to create relational databases with two linked tables – with referential integrity

★ SQL operations including SELECT FROM/WHERE, ORDER BY, UPDATE, DELETE

★ equi-join in SQL.

Database development using Microsoft Access

Other database development programs are available; however, the majority of schools currently use MS Access for this.

Beginning a new database

When you open Access, click on Blank database.

When you start a new database, MS Access requires you to save the file right away. However, the folder it wishes to save into as a default may not be the folder you wish to use. Click the folder icon to navigate to the place you wish to save your file. Don't forget to name your file too. Then click Create.

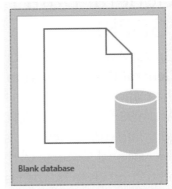

Blank database

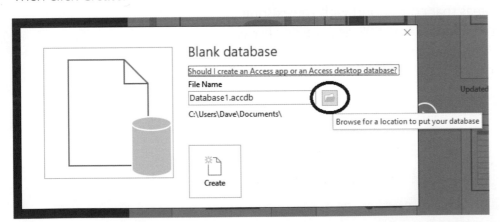

Now your file is opened, with a table already created, and the table is open in Datasheet view. If you are using this chapter to work through as a step-by-step tutorial, it is better to close this table and then right-click the table in the pane to the left and delete the table for now.

Creating a table

An 'entity' from the design stage is created as a 'table' in the implementation stage. To do this you go to the Create tab and click on Table. The new table will open in Datasheet view. In fact, to begin adding fields to your table, you are better to switch to Design view at the top-left.

Once in Design view you can take the 'attributes' from the design stage and add them as 'fields' in MS Access. MS Access automatically names the first field 'ID' with the data type 'Autonumber' and makes this the primary key. You can use the Key icon on the toolbar to remove or add a field as primary key for that table. Below is the Design view for a table about cars.

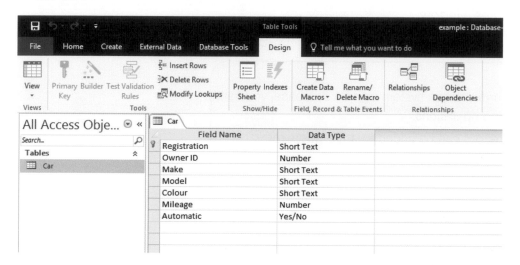

You may wish to refer back to the table on validation in Chapter 9, page 105 to implement validation on the fields in Design view.

Linking tables

To link tables in MS Access, you have to ensure that:

- each table has a primary key
- one table contains a field that is the primary key of the other table (a foreign key)
- the foreign key has the same data type as the primary key it will link to
- there is no data in the foreign key field that doesn't have identical data in the primary key field in the other table, to match up to.

If any of these conditions are not met, you cannot link tables with **referential integrity**.

Referential integrity means that the data held in the foreign key field must refer to an entry in the primary key field of the linked table. This is a way of preventing errors in the data.

Assuming the above conditions have been met, to link two tables you must first close the tables and any queries that use those tables. Next go to the Database Tools tab and select Relationships.

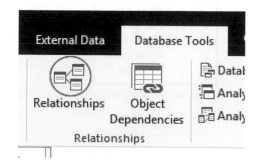

Now you have to double-click each of your two table names to add them, then click Close. Now drag the foreign key field name onto the name of the primary key field from the other table. When you let go, you will see a dialog box pop up. Tick the box to Enforce Referential Integrity and click Create.

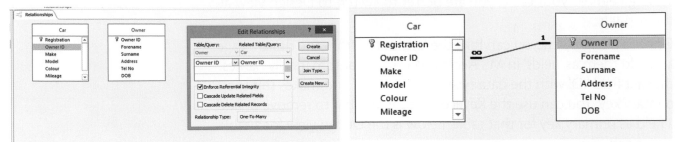

Save and close the Relationships window.

Once you have created your information system using a database, you can use it to carry out the following operations.

* **Adding records**: a new record can be added to a file when, for example, a new car comes onto the market.
* **Simple search** (a search on one field): a search is also called a query or a find. A simple search on the database file involves searching on one field only, for example, search for those records where the first_name field = "Jack".
* **Sort on one field**: you can arrange, or sort, the records into order based on the contents of one field, for example, sort on the second_name field in ascending order (from a to z).
* **Complex search** (a search on more than one field): a complex search is based on two or more fields, for example, a search for those records where the first_name field = "Jean" AND the second_name field = "Brown".
* **Sort on more than one field**: this is where two or more fields are used to arrange the data, for example, sort class file on grade field and second_name field, both in ascending order. This will sort the records so that the grades are in order, with all those with grade 1 followed by grade 2 etc. and each of these groups is sorted into alphabetical order of second name/surname. The screenshot below shows an example of this.

Grade	Surname
1	Carrick
1	Dorward
1	Howard
1	Thomson
2	Campbell
2	McCulloch
2	Robertson
2	Shearer

Queries

Queries are used to extract information from the database. Later we will look at using **SQL** to perform queries. However, the usual way to search or sort the database within MS Access is to go to the Create tab and choose Query Design.

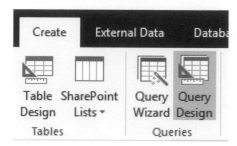

Now you have to double-click table names to add them, then click Close. The Criteria row is used to type in terms that you wish to search for, and the Sort row is used to choose the order to sort on a field. Then click Run in the Design tab to see the query results.

Example

Here is the Design view for a search for all automatic cars with mileage under 100 000. The results are sorted by the owner's date of birth with the oldest owner first.

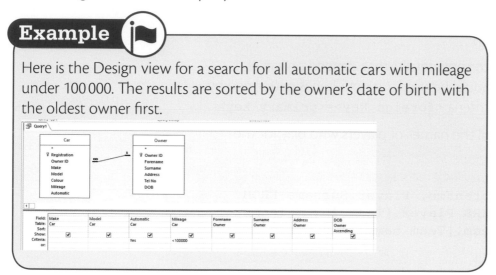

SQL operations

SQL stands for Structured Query Language. This language is how online shops or social media websites are likely to interact with their databases. It isn't usual to use SQL within MS Access in an office or workplace; however, it does allow the use of SQL, which is ideal for you to use to practise and learn basic SQL.

Queries using SQL

The syntax for a SQL query is:

```
SELECT <fields> FROM <tables> WHERE <search
criteria> ORDER BY <field> ASC/DESC, <field>
ASC/DESC;
```

When selecting fields you should use **dot notation** (for example, `Player.[Player ID]`) to indicate what table the field has come from. Square brackets are put around field names that have a space. To select all the fields from a table you can simply use an asterisk (*) for example:

```
SELECT * FROM Team;
```

As you can see from the above example on page 111, both WHERE and ORDER BY are optional.

Search criteria should include the field name. For example:

```
SELECT * FROM Player WHERE Player.Forename =
"David" ORDER BY Player.Surname ASC;
```

will show all fields from the Player table but only those records where the player's first name is David. The results will be sorted in ascending alphabetical order of surname.

Search criteria may make use of the logical operators such as AND, OR, > (greater than) and < (less than).

When the query is intended to show results that depend on tables being linked, an '**equi-join**' should be used. An equi-join is performed by adding as part of the search criteria `<foreign key>=<primary key>`.

Here is an example to show all the names of players who play for the team called George Street:

```
SELECT Player.Forename, Player.Surname FROM
Player, Team WHERE Player.[Team ID] = Team.
[Team ID] AND Team.[Team name] = "George
Street";
```

Editing the database using SQL

SQL can be used to add records, change records or delete records.

Adding records

To add records, the syntax is:

```
INSERT INTO <table> (<field>, <field>, <field>,
…) VALUES (<data>, <data>, <data>, …);
```

For example, to add a new record to the Team table for a team called Prestwick, you would use:

```
INSERT INTO Team ([Team ID], [Team name])
VALUES (96, "Prestwick");
```

Changing records

To change records, the syntax is:

```
UPDATE <table> SET <field> = <data>, <field> =
data, <field> = data, … WHERE <criteria>;
```

For example, to change all players currently on team number 23 to play instead for the new team:

```
UPDATE Player SET Player.[Team ID]=96 WHERE
Player.[Team ID]=23;
```

Deleting records

To delete records, the syntax is:

```
DELETE FROM <table> WHERE <criteria>;
```

For example, to delete team number 23 from the Team table:

```
DELETE FROM Team WHERE Team.[Team ID]=23;
```

Questions

1 Show the correct SQL statement to show all fields and all records from a table called 'Charity'.
2 Explain the effect of the SQL statement:

```
SELECT * FROM Charity WHERE
Focus="Homelessness";
```

3 Show the correct SQL statement to show all records from a table called 'Charity' but only the 'Name' and 'Focus' fields.
4 Show the correct SQL statement to show all fields and all records from the table called 'Charity' sorted in alphabetical order of the charity name.
5 Explain the effect of the SQL statement:

```
DELETE * FROM Charity;
```

6 Show the correct SQL statement to delete all records from the Charity table that focus on animals.

Testing and evaluation (database)

Testing SQL operations

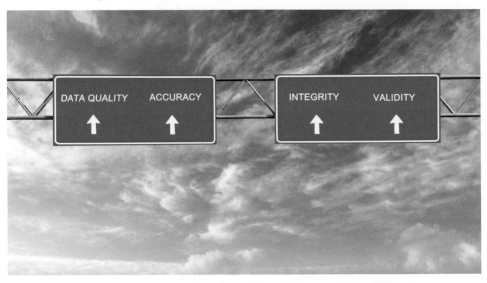

Just one SQL statement run on a database containing a very high number of records could end up altering or showing a lot of data. To ensure you have constructed the statement correctly, it is a good idea to try it out on a version of the database with a small number of records first to check it.

There is no strict format for noting your testing, but it is good practice to note what results you expect, then run the query and note what results you actually get and comment on any differences.

Remember, if there are differences perhaps your SQL statement is wrong, or perhaps your expectations were wrong!

Example

Testing for query to show cars with mileage less than 80 000		
SQL statement: SELECT * FROM Cars WHERE Mileage <= 80000		
Expected result	**Actual result**	**Comment**
Three records (Ford Focus, Ford Fiesta, Honda Accord)	Four results (Citroen C1, Ford Focus, Ford Fiesta, Honda Accord)	SQL should contain '<'instead of '<='

Evaluating a database solution

Fitness for purpose

The developers of the database will go back to the statement about the problem that was agreed at the analysis stage and compare this with the database that has actually been created.

If the database has been successfully proven to meet all of the points given in the problem or detailed in the statement about the problem that was agreed at the analysis stage, then it can be said to be fit for purpose.

If you are writing an evaluation of fitness for purpose, be sure to mention:
● each individual thing that the database was required to do
● that it does each of those things
● how you know that it does each of them (refer to your testing).

Accuracy of output

The **accuracy of the output** is your evaluation of your queries. Are the results produced the same as the results you expected? You can use your testing to provide evidence that the output from your database is accurate.

Evaluating an SQL statement

You may be asked to evaluate an SQL statement, in which case, as well as stating whether the SQL statement shown correctly performs the action it is intended to, you must also state whether or not the SQL statement is fit for purpose.

Section 4 Web Design and Development

Chapter 12
Analysis and design (web)

What you should know

By the end of this chapter you should **know** and **understand** how to:

★ identify the end-user and functional requirements of a website problem

★ describe and exemplify the website structure with a **home page**, a maximum of four linked multimedia pages, and any necessary external links

★ describe, exemplify and implement, taking into account end-user requirements, effective user-interface design (visual layout and readability) using wire-framing including navigational links, consistency across multiple pages, relative vertical positioning of the media displayed and file formats of the media (text, graphics, video, and audio)

★ describe and identify the implications for individuals and businesses of the Copyright, Designs and Patents Act (1988) relating to web content (text, graphics, video, and audio)

★ describe, exemplify and implement low-fidelity prototypes from a wireframe design

★ compare audio standard file formats WAV and MP3 in terms of compression, quality, and file size

★ compare bit-mapped graphic standard file formats JPEG, GIF and PNG in terms of compression, animation, **transparency** and colour depth

★ describe the factors affecting file size and quality, relating to resolution, colour depth and sampling rate

★ describe the need for compression.

Analysing a website problem

Functional requirements

Functional requirements are those which fulfil the reasons that the website is to be created. These will include the different pages that must be created, the information that must be shown on each, the media (images, video or sound) to be used on each page and the structure of the site (which pages have hyperlinks and where those links point to).

End-user requirements

End-user requirements are those facilities or features that have to be included to ensure that users are able to access the information on the web pages and make use of any features such as media.

Internal and external hyperlinks

A hyperlink allows a user to click an image or text to take them to a different web page, or sometimes to download a file or begin a new email to a certain address. An **internal hyperlink** points to a page or file on the same website. An **external hyperlink** points to a page or file on another website.

An external hyperlink will always use the full URL of where it links to. URL stands for Uniform Resource Locator, an example of a URL would be https://www.sqa.org.uk/sqa/48477.html.

Example 🚩

A new children's television programme based on a graphic novel has begun to air and is becoming increasingly popular. A website is required to allow fans to find out more information about the four main characters and the actors who play them. The **home page** should contain a description of the show and an image of each of the four characters with their names beneath them. Each of the images should be clickable so that the user can use the ⇨

---

image to access the page about that character. The home page should also have an external link to the website about the graphic novel that inspired the programme's creation. Across the website, the font size should be 14 point or larger and have dark-coloured text on a light-coloured background to ensure it can be easily read, even by young children. The site should avoid green and red as these can be difficult for colour-blind individuals. Each character page should have an image and a text summary of that character. The page should also have embedded audio of an interview with the actor that can be downloaded using a **standard file format**. Each character page should have a link back to the home page.

For the above example, the functional requirements are:

- a home page with an **internal hyperlink** on four separate images to four different pages
- an **external hyperlink** from the home page to the graphic novel's website
- on the home page, text of the names of the characters (lined up beneath their picture) and text of a summary of the programme
- on each character page, a hyperlink back to the home page
- on each character page, text description of the character
- on each character page, an embedded audio player to play an interview
- on each character page, a hyperlink to download a media file of the interview in MP3 or WAV format.

The end-user requirements are:

- 14 pt font size or greater
- contrasting colours of dark text and light background
- avoidance of green or red
- access hyperlinks
- play interview
- download interview.

Website design

Navigational structure

This is a simple diagram showing all pages on the site and how they link to each other (internal hyperlinks) or how they link to other websites (external hyperlinks).

Example 🚩

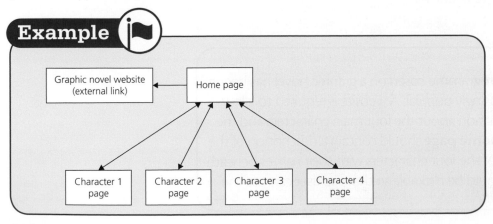

User interface design

A key part of creating an information system is to design a user interface.

Target audience

When you are designing an interface for your information system it is important to know as much as possible about the type of user it is being designed for. There are many things to think about such as the user's age, their interests, their lifestyles, their level of experience, knowledge and skills.

The more information you have about your target audience, the better you will be able to design an interface that they will find easy to use.

Designing a user interface

A well-designed user interface will pay attention to:

1 **Visual layout**

   This means:

   ● ensuring elements are positioned on the screen so that they line up vertically
   ● avoiding using inappropriate or gaudy colours
   ● balancing the colours
   ● keeping the screen uncluttered
   ● avoiding using too many animation special effects.

2 Navigation

   How the user moves from one screen to another.

3 Consistency
This involves using the same:
- terms throughout
- sounds to alert, for example, an input error
- mouse action or command to produce the same action
- font and font size
- graphics style and size
- navigation bar in the same location on each web page
- text alignment.

4 Interactivity
This involves using:
- feedback to step users through a process or alert them to errors
- hotspots to trigger actions
- clear links with meaningful link text
- interactive animations
- video clips
- sound files
- polls or quizzes.

5 **Readability**
This means paying attention to:
- text size
- font
- colour balance
- use of headings and sub-headings.

Wireframe

In National 5 you will design the user interface for programs and web pages using a wireframe. A wireframe is a labelled plan of what will be on the screen.

Here is a checklist of what to include in a wireframe for a web page:
- page title in address bar
- areas that will show text and a short statement of what text they will show
- areas where the user will input data
- areas that may change to show output of data
- areas that link to another page/file/screen
- any sound that will be heard
- any image file that will be included
- font information (size, font name, formatting, colour)
- all colour information.

Example 📐

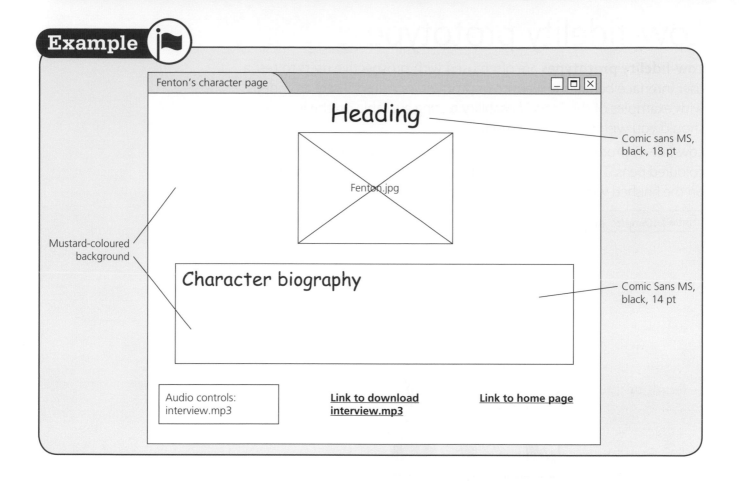

The Copyright, Designs and Patents Act (1988)

When designing and creating any product, including a web page, it is important that any work that is not your own is only included with the permission of the creator. This law applies to text, audio recordings, images (even those found through an image search on a search engine!), videos, animations and designs. Most creators will expect a form of payment in order for their permission to be given, but some require only that you acknowledge them as the creator within your work.

The **Copyright, Designs and Patents Act** also deals with computer software, which is now protected by law for 50 years after it is published. The Act makes it illegal to:

- make unauthorised (pirate) copies of software
- run pirated software
- transmit software over telecommunications links and copy it
- run multiple copies of software if only one copy was purchased
- give, lend or sell copies of bought software unless a licence to do so is granted.

Low-fidelity prototype

Low-fidelity prototypes are often used with prospective users to test a user interface before the website or product is created. There are videos with examples of this kind of usability testing available on the internet should you wish to see it in action.

Low-fidelity prototypes are drawn with paper or card and pens, sometimes coloured pens. They will include text and images that are planned to appear on the finished web pages and areas for user interaction.

Fenton's character page

Fenton Quinn

Fenton is the only son of Harvard and Lily Quinn. He makes his own choices and they aren't always ones that others agree with, but he doesn't care. Sometimes he acts as the leader of the group, but just as often plays the joker. He doesn't take life too seriously and enjoys making fun of his friend. However, he is also very brave. Fenton stands up for his friends and has helped them out of one or two scrapes in the past.

Download Interview

Back to home

Hints & tips

'Fidelity' means faithfulness. They are called low-fidelity prototypes because they needn't look a lot like the finished product; the look is not faithful to the completed version.

Questions ❓

1. Explain the difference between an internal hyperlink and an external hyperlink.
2. Suggest one possible problem that may occur when your website contains an external hyperlink.
3. Asif uses a photo taken by Jodie on his website. Jodie says that this is ok. Has Asif broken the Copyright, Designs and Patents Act (1988)?

Standard file formats

A standard file format is a file type that is widely used for saving data and so is likely to be able to be opened by a wide range of programs. For example, the free sound-editing software Audacity saves its projects as AUP files. These files are *not* compatible with other programs and so are not a suitable format to use for saving sound files to be accessed from a web page. Instead suitable standard file formats would be WAV or MP3 (either of which you can use to export a project from, in Audacity).

The need for compression

When a company has a website, it must be hosted on a server. The more space the site takes up on the server, the more costly it is to run the website, because more backing storage capacity must be bought (and maintained) or rented. Uncompressed video files take up an extremely large amount of space; uncompressed sound files take up a large amount of space and even uncompressed image files will take up more space than they really need to.

Users accessing media files that are not compressed will find that they take a long time to download; because of this, companies could even lose customers to their rivals who have used compression, or users in areas without fast internet connection speeds could miss out on content.

There are two kinds of **compression**: **lossless**, which compresses without losing quality, and **lossy**, which sacrifices quality for a smaller file size.

Comparison of audio standard file formats

	WAV	MP3
Compression	Lossless	Lossy
Quality	Excellent, identical to the original sound	Very good, designed so that the user doesn't notice the data that has been removed (removes the quieter of any two similar sounds, removes frequencies outside of human hearing range)
File size	High for sound	Reasonably low

Comparison of bitmap standard file formats

	JPEG	GIF	PNG
Compression	Lossy, adjustable	Lossless (low file size is achieved by limited colour depth)	Lossless
Animation	Not possible	Possible	Not possible
Transparency	Not possible	Individual pixels can be fully transparent or not at all	Individual pixels can have their level of **transparency** set. Transparency level can vary.
Colour depth	24 bit allows 2^{24} = 16 777 216 colours	8 bit allows 2^8 = 256 colours	24 bit allows 2^{24} = 16 777 216 colours

Other factors affecting file size

Even before compression, when creating the original uncompressed media files, it is important to understand some of the features of these files that can affect the file size.

Colour depth (bit depth) and resolution affect the file size of images. This has already been covered in 'Bit-mapped storage', Chapter 6, page 94.

Uncompressed audio file size

Sound in the physical world travels as waves. These waves can vary in frequency (which affects the pitch of the sound we hear) and in amplitude (the volume of the sound we hear). To convert this analogue sound wave into numbers in binary, the wave is sampled regularly. This means the numerical value of the amplitude is saved as a binary number. The wave is sampled so often that the numbers stored, called samples, can be used to play back the original sound. The number of times the wave is sampled in one second is called the sampling rate. It is measured in hertz (Hz), but more often converted into kilohertz (KHz).

CD quality sound is 44 100 samples per second: a **sampling rate** of 44 100 Hz or 44.1KHz.

The higher the sampling rate, the higher the quality of the sound, but also this means a bigger file size, as more samples are being stored.

Questions ?

4 When making media files available for download from a website, why should they be stored in a standard file format?
5 Give two reasons why media files made available for download from a website should be compressed.
6 Which image file formats support transparency?
7 Explain two differences between GIF and PNG.
8 What effect would decreasing the resolution of an image have on file size?
9 What effect would increasing the sample rate of a sound have on file size?

Chapter 13

Implementation (web)

What you should know

By the end of this chapter you should **know** and **understand** how to:

★ describe, exemplify and implement the HTML tags for HTML, head, title, body, heading, paragraph, DIV, link, anchor, IMG, audio, video, ordered lists, unordered lists and hyperlinks (internal and external) using **relative** and **absolute addressing**

★ describe, exemplify and implement internal and external cascading style sheets (CSS) selectors, classes and IDs with properties text (including font family, font size, 'color' and alignment) and background colour

★ describe and identify JavaScript coding related to mouse events onmouseover and onmouseout.

The **browser** receives the text of the web page file and translates this into what is seen on screen. The text will include **HTML**, and may also include CSS and/or JavaScript.

HTML

HTML stands for Hypertext Markup Language. It was originally designed to tell the web browser what the structure of a web page should be, although it does also contain instructions for some formatting of the text as well. HTML does this by having tags inside pointy brackets that are positioned around the text that will appear on the web page. The tags are not case-sensitive.

Basic page structure

The HTML on a page will begin with a `<HTML>` tag and end with a `</HTML>` tag. There will be two main sections, first a head section and then a body section.

The head section

The head section will begin with `<HEAD>` and end with `</HEAD>`. The head section contains information about the web page. One HTML tag you will use in the head section is the title tag. It is used to set the page title that will appear inside the tab on the browser. This title does not appear in the body of the page. The syntax is:

```
<TITLE>Page title here</TITLE>
```

This will produce:

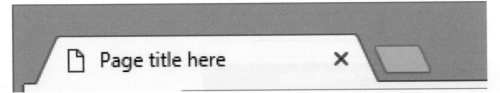

Another tag that may be used within the head section is the `<LINK>` tag. This has no closing tag. It is used to specify an **external stylesheet** (a CSS file) to be used to apply formatting to the web page. You will learn more about CSS later in this chapter. To link to an external stylesheet called `home_page_styles.css`, the following syntax would be used:

```
<LINK rel="stylesheet" type="text/css"
href="home_page_styles.css">
```

The body section

The body section begins with `<BODY>` and ends with `</BODY>`. This section will contain all of the content that is actually displayed in the web page.

Headings

The syntax for a heading tag is:

```
<H3>Heading text here</H3>
```

This will produce:

Heading text here

There are six headings available, from `<H1>` to `<H6>`. The numbers indicate a scale of priority, `<H1>` is the most important heading, and `<H6>` is the least important heading.

Paragraphs

Each paragraph always begins on a new line within the web page. Paragraphs begin with `<P>` and end with `</P>`. The syntax is:

```
<P>Paragraph text here</P>
```

Numbered lists and bullet points

A numbered list begins with the tag `<OL>` and ends with `</OL>`. This stands for **ordered list**. Within these tags each numbered item should appear within `<LI>` and `</LI>` tags. This stands for list item.

```
<OL>
<LI>item one</LI>
<LI>item two</LI>
<LI>item three</LI>
</OL>
```

produces

1. item one
2. item two
3. item three

`<OL start="10">` can be used to start the list from ten.

A list with bullet points begins with `<UL>` and ends with `</UL>`. This stands for **unordered list**. Within these tags, again, each item should appear within `<LI>` and `</LI>` tags.

```
<UL>
<LI>item one</LI>
<LI>item two</LI>
<LI>item three</LI>
</UL>
```

produces

- item one
- item two
- item three

Each list will be slightly indented from the previous text.

Hints & tips

When typing the HTML text of a web page, pressing return will take a new line within your editor, but it doesn't take a new line in the web page shown in the browser! New lines have to be indicated with tags such as `<BR>` or using paragraph markers.

1 Which tag should appear at the very end of all the HTML in a web page document?
2 At National 5 level, which two opening tags are the only opening tags you should see in the head section?
3 How many different heading tags are there in HTML?
4 What will the browser show if the following HTML appears in the body section?

```
<OL>
<LI>Alan</LI>
<UL>
<LI>Carrie</LI>
<LI>Alynna</LI>
</UL>
<LI>Bob</LI>
</OL>
```

Key points !

Relative and absolute addressing

An absolute web address specifies exactly on which server the web page is stored and directs you to that server. Absolute paths *always* include the domain name of the website, including http://www. This points to the server on which it is stored. The two addresses below are examples of this:

* http://www.bbc.co.uk/sport/football/scottish-premiership
* http://www.mysite.com/help/articles/how-do-i-set-up-a-webpage. HTML

On the other hand, a relative web address links a web page to other web pages on a single website (using internal hyperlinks). Relative links only point to a file or a file path, often on the computer on which it is being developed. This is used when developers construct a site in one place and then publish it to another place. An example of this is:

* help/articles/how-do-i-set-up-a-webpage.HTML

This also applies to links to media files used on the web page.

Media

Images

To show an image on the web page the `<IMG>` tag is used. It has no closing tag but does require the 'src' attribute to be set to show the location of the image, using either relative or absolute addressing. The `<IMG>` tag also has optional attributes which include height (in pixels), width (in pixels).

Example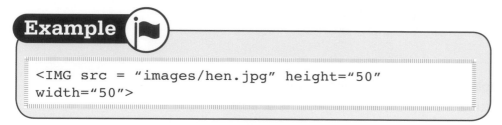

```
<IMG src = "images/hen.jpg" height="50"
width="50">
```

Audio

Audio begins with `<AUDIO>` and ends with `</AUDIO>`. The opening tag has one optional attribute, 'controls', which will show icons to allow users to play, pause, adjust volume or drag a slider to a different point in the audio track currently playing. It will also show the time that the slider is currently at.

Within the `<AUDIO>` and `</AUDIO>` tags there will be one or more `<SOURCE>` tags. The `<SOURCE>` tag has no closing tag, and has two attributes: 'src' to hold the link to the audio file to be played, and 'type' to indicate the file format that the audio file is in. The syntax is:

```
<AUDIO controls>
  <SOURCE src="cluck.wav" type="audio/wav">
  <SOURCE src="cluck.mp3" type="audio/mpeg">
Your browser does not support this audio
element.
</AUDIO>
```

The effect of the above example is that the audio controls will be shown and play the file cluck.wav unless the browser being used is unable to play WAV files in this way. If the browser is unable to play WAV files, it will instead show audio controls and play the MP3 file cluck.mp3. If the browser is also unable to play MP3 files, then the text 'Your browser does not support this audio element.' will be shown.

Video

Video begins with `<VIDEO>` and ends with `</VIDEO>`. The opening tag has three optional attributes: 'controls', which will show the time the video is currently at along with icons to allow users to play, pause, adjust volume or drag a slider to a different point in the video currently playing; 'height', which sets the height of the video display area in pixels; and 'width', which sets the breadth of the video display area in pixels.

Within the <VIDEO> and </VIDEO> tags there will be one or more <SOURCE> tags. The <SOURCE> tag has no closing tag, and has two attributes: 'src' to hold the link to the video file to be played, and 'type' to indicate the file format that the video file is in. The syntax is:

```
<VIDEO controls>
  <SOURCE src="farmyard.ogg" type="video/ogg">
  <SOURCE src="farmyard.mp4" type="video/mp4">
Your browser does not support this video
element.
</VIDEO>
```

The effect of the above example is that the video controls will be shown and play the file farmyard.ogg unless the browser being used is unable to play OGG files in this way. If the browser is unable to play OGG files, it will instead show video controls and play the MP4 file farmyard.mp4. If the browser is also unable to play MP4 files, then the text 'Your browser does not support this video element.' will be shown.

Sections/Divisions

A web page is commonly split up into parts with each part containing a few headings and paragraphs. The <DIV> and </DIV> tags allow these separate sections to be defined. This in turn allows different CSS (or HTML) formatting to be applied to different sections.

Key points !

The id attribute

The id attribute can be added to any HTML tag to give that element a unique identifier. This identifier can then be used as an anchor (see below) or when applying CSS or JavaScript. For example, you might use <DIV id="Introduction"> as an opening tag for a section to which you wish to assign the unique identifier 'Introduction'. When using an id, the same id cannot be applied to more than one element.

The class attribute

The class attribute can be added to any HTML tag to indicate that that element is part of a certain group of elements. Each element in that group will have the same class assigned to it. This makes it easy to apply the same formatting to a group of elements using CSS. An element can be part of more than one class, and the same class is likely to appear on multiple elements. For example, all paragraphs in the first section of a page may begin with <P class="first"> or all headings which feature names of animals may begin with <H2 class="animal">.

Hyperlinks and anchors

A hyperlink allows a user to click an image or text to take them to a different web page, or sometimes to download a file or begin a new email to a certain address. When combined with **anchors**, a hyperlink can be clicked to take users to another place on the same web page.

The syntax for a hyperlink is:

```
<A href="address of the web page or file to be
linked to">Link text or image</A>
```

For example:

```
Click <A href="http://www.hoddereducation.
co.uk">here</A> for more revision books.
```

is an external hyperlink (therefore using absolute addressing) that will show:

Click <u>here</u> for more revision books.

In a hyperlink using an anchor, the address specified in the 'href' attribute will end with the '#' symbol and then the unique identifier assigned to the element on the target page that you wish to link to (see *The id attribute* above).

So, if the Hodder Education page contained a section with the id Computing_Science, the link could have the syntax:

```
Click <A href="http://www.hoddereducation.
co.uk#Computing_Science">here</A> for Computing
Science books.
```

Larger Wikipedia articles use anchors to provide the links within the Contents section.

Questions

5 Explain the difference between relative and absolute addressing.
6 Which tag is used to show an image?
7 What effect does adding the 'controls' attribute to the `<AUDIO>` tag have?
8 Explain the difference between a class and an id.
9 When a hyperlink is using an anchor, which character comes before the id of the element that you want to link to?

Cascading style sheets (CSS)

Cascading style sheets (CSS) were created to apply formatting to the content of web pages, to improve their appearance. This was because HTML was only intended to provide very basic options in terms of formatting. CSS can be external, internal or in-line. External styles are applied by the browser first, then internal styles are applied (possibly over-ruling styles from the external stylesheet) then in-line styles are applied (again possibly over-ruling styles that came before).

Key points

External stylesheets have all the styling rules stored in a separate text document sent along with the web page. One stylesheet can be applied to multiple pages on a site, making it easy to have a consistent look and feel across all the pages on the same website. This can save development time as the styles are only created within one document. An added advantage of this is that only one stylesheet need be downloaded for all the pages, which can improve web page load times. Each web page must use the `<LINK>` tag in the head section to indicate the location of the stylesheet, for example:

```
<LINK rel="stylesheet" type="text/css"
    href="home_page_styles.css">
```

Internal stylesheets have all the styling rules contained within the head section of the HTML page. This can ensure consistent styling across one page, and can be useful when you want one page on the site to have a different look and feel to the others.

In-line CSS are used when a styling rule appears within the HTML tag that the rule will apply to. This is useful when you wish to make individual elements of the page have a different look and feel to the rest of the page.

CSS rules

A rule always begins with a selector. The selector is the name of the element, class or id that the rule applies to. The selector is followed by a declaration containing the property to be set and the value it is to be set to.

A rule that applies to all H1 elements:

```
H1 { color:blue; font-size:20px;}
```

A rule that applies to all elements of the class called 'first':

```
.first { text-align:left; font-family:Arial;}
```

Hints & tips

A property in CSS is a bit like an attribute in HTML. It is some aspect of the element(s) selected.

A rule that applies to the element with the id 'Introduction':

```
#Introduction { background-color:yellow;
    color:#ff0000;}
```

There are five properties that you have to be able to use at National 5 level and these are detailed in the table below.

Property	Effect	Example
color	Sets the font colour, supports colour names or hex codes	color: magenta;
font-size	Sets the font size	font-size: 14px;
font-family	Sets the font you wish to use if it is available. If this font is not supported by the browser, a similar alternative will be used	font-family: Tahoma;
text-align	Sets the alignment/justification of the text	text-align: center;
background-color	Sets the background colour of the area, supports colour names or hex codes	background-color: #ff6347;

Questions

10 Explain two advantages of using an external CSS stylesheet over an internal CSS.
11 What HTML code would appear in the head section to apply an external stylesheet called 'superstyle.css'?
12 Show the correct CSS rule to set all H2 headings to a font size of 18px.
13 Explain the effect of the CSS rule:

```
.description { text-align: center; font-
    family: Calibri;}
```

14 Show the correct CSS rule to set the element with id 'special' to have a background colour of green.

JavaScript

JavaScript is a scripting language that allows programs to be run by the browser as part of the web page. It is often used to add an area where the user can interact with the web page.

At National 5 level you need to be able to describe and identify the mouse events **onmouseover** and **onmouseout**. What this means is that when the mouse pointer moves over an element, one subprogram is run. When the pointer leaves the element, a different subprogram is run.

Often onmouseover is used to change the formatting of the element in some way, and then onmouseout is used to return the element to its original formatting.

Creating the subprogram

The subprogram for each event is often created in the head section of the HTML code of the web page, but will also work in the body section. The JavaScript subprograms must be placed between the <SCRIPT> and </SCRIPT> tags.

The subprogram must be told which element it is going to edit. This can be done by using the id assigned to the element, or by using the element as a parameter (an argument). The first example below uses the id, the second uses a parameter.

Calling the subprogram

The subprogram that has been written (between <SCRIPT> and </SCRIPT>) must still be called when the appropriate event (onmouseover or onmouseout) happens to the appropriate element. To cause the subprogram to be called, the element must have an attribute called 'onmouseover' or 'onmouseout' set to the name of the subprogram that is going to be called.

Example 🚩

Example 1

```
<HTML>
<HEAD>
<SCRIPT>
function mouseOverExample() {
document.getElementById("intro_heading").style.
color="red";
}
function mouseOutExample() {
document.getElementById("intro_heading").style.
color = "black";
}
</SCRIPT>
</HEAD>
<BODY>
<H1 id="intro_heading" onmouseover="mouseOverExa
mple()" onmouseout="mouseOutExample()">Introduct
ion</H1>
</BODY>
</HTML>
```

⇨

```
<HTML>
<HEAD>
<SCRIPT>
function mouseOverExample(target) {
target.style.color="red";
}
function mouseOutExample(target) {
target.style.color = "black";
}
</SCRIPT>
</HEAD>
<BODY>
<H1 onmouseover="mouseOverExample(this)" onmouse
out="mouseOutExample(this)">Introduction</H1>
</BODY>
</HTML>
```

The above examples use '**style.color**' to set the font colour.

JavaScript style properties	
.style.color	Sets the font colour
.style.textAlign	Sets the alignment/justification of the text
.style.fontSize	Sets the font size
.style.fontFamily	Sets the font you wish to use if it is available. If this font is not supported by the browser, a similar alternative will be used
.style.backgroundColor	Sets the background colour

You will not have to write any JavaScript, only recognise and interpret what it is doing.

Testing and evaluation (web)

Testing a website

It is important to use your testing to ensure that you have met the end-user and functional requirements of the problem. To test the user interface, you should check each page of your website against the wireframe plan that you made of that page and ensure that they match. You should check that all text can be read and is neither too small nor lacking in contrast with the background colour. You should listen to each piece of audio and watch each video to ensure that they play correctly. You should check that each image displays, is of the correct size and is in the correct position on the page.

Testing

Hyperlinks can be checked by noting where you expect each link to take the user, then clicking the link and noting where the hyperlink actually takes the user, and commenting on whether or not the reality matches your expectations. This is similar to testing a program or a database query.

Finally, you should comment on the **consistency** of your pages.
- Do they all have the same or similar colour scheme?
- Do they all have the same or similar layout?
- Are the font types/sizes/formatting/colours for corresponding areas on different pages still the same?
- Do the hyperlinks appear in the same position across multiple pages, particularly those links where the destination will be the same, regardless of which page they appear on, for example, 'Back to home'?
- Do audio/video/images appear in a consistent position across all the pages?

Evaluating a website

You will have to evaluate the fitness for purpose of the website. This involves going back to the original problem and explaining that you have met each thing you were asked to do, how you have accomplished each of those tasks, and how you know and can prove that each of those aspects of the problem have been solved. You should refer to the end-user requirements, the functional requirements and to your testing.

Preparation for the assignment

What to expect

The assignment is designed to assess your skills in the practical application of the National 5 course content.

The assignment will have 50 marks available. This is combined with the 110 mark question paper element, providing a total of 160 marks for National 5. This means that the assignment is worth just over 30% of your overall mark for this course.

The assignment will feature a section on database design and development, a section on software design and development, and a section on web design and development. Each section will have a problem set within a context or situation. It is likely that the situations for the three sections will not be related.

The section on software design and development will always be the largest, worth 25 marks – half of the available marks for the assignment. The other two sections will be worth between 10 and 15 marks, but will total up to 25 marks so that they together account for the other half of the available marks.

Across the three sections, you will be required to demonstrate your skills in analysis, design, implementation, testing and evaluation. However, each of these skills also has a mark allocation. There are 30 marks for implementation and 5 marks for each of the others. This means that it is likely that if you are given the design for the programming and web design problems, then you will have to complete the design for the database problem; or if you are asked to complete part of the analysis for the web design problem and the database problem, then you will be given the analysis for the programming problem.

There is a new assignment released each year, valid only for that year. You are allowed a total of eight hours to complete the assignment. The assignment is sent away to the SQA to be marked. It will not be reviewed by your teacher and returned to you for improvement. There is no word limit or page limit.

What help am I allowed?

The assignment is an open-book assessment. This means that you can look at previous work that you have completed (on paper or in files). This is often the best way to remind yourself of a certain detail that you have forgotten. You are allowed to look at textbooks, so can have this book beside you as you undertake the assignment. You are not allowed to look at the work of another candidate. The teacher is only allowed to help you to access the resources (e.g. files) required for the tasks within the assignment.

Am I suitably prepared?

Below is a checklist of the activities that you may be asked to undertake as part of the assignment. For each one, ensure that you have an example that has been checked by your teacher that you are able to refer back to during the assignment. You may wish to ask your teacher for extra practice on any area below in which you feel unsure.

Analysis

☐ Identify the purpose of a program from a description
☐ Identify the functional requirements of a program from a description
☐ Identify the inputs, processes and outputs of a program from a description
☐ Identify the end-user requirements of a database from a description
☐ Identify the functional requirements of a database from a description
☐ Identify the end-user requirements of a website from a description
☐ Identify the functional requirements of a website from a description

Design

☐ Identify the data types and data structures from a description or analysis for a program
☐ Interpret or create a structure diagram for a program
☐ Interpret or create a flowchart for a program
☐ Interpret or create pseudocode for a program
☐ Interpret or create a wireframe for a program
☐ Interpret, complete or create an entity relationship diagram for a database
☐ Interpret or complete a data dictionary for a database
☐ Interpret, complete or create the design of a query for a database
☐ Identify the implications of current data protection laws on the implementation of a database
☐ Interpret or complete a diagram showing the structure of a website
☐ Interpret or create a wireframe for a website
☐ Interpret or create a low-fidelity prototype for a web page
☐ Identify the implications of the Copyright, Designs and Patents Act 1988 relating to a website
☐ Comment on compression and characteristics of standard file formats for media files to be used on a website

Implementation

☐ Make use of both variables and one-dimensional arrays within a program
☐ Make use of data types character, string, integer, real and Boolean within a program
☐ Perform calculations including addition, subtraction, multiplication, division and exponentiation within a program

☐ Make use of conditional statements and conditional loops including <, >, ≤, ≥, =, ≠, AND, OR and NOT within a program

☐ Make use of fixed loops within a program

☐ Implement the input validation standard algorithm within a program

☐ Implement the running total within a loop standard algorithm within a program

☐ Implement traversing a one-dimensional array standard algorithm within a program

☐ Create a database with two tables, with appropriate fields and data types

☐ Link tables with referential integrity

☐ Complete SQL statements to query or edit records within a database, including equi-join

☐ Create HTML documents including:
- a title
- headings
- paragraphs
- DIV tags
- images
- audio
- video
- ordered and unordered lists
- hyperlinks
- anchors
- classes and ids
- linking to an external CSS

☐ Create internal or external CSS including:
- setting text colour
- setting font
- setting text size
- setting text alignment
- setting background colour

☐ Describe JavaScript coding initiated by mouse event onmouseover or onmouseout

Testing

☐ Make use of normal, extreme and exceptional test data within a test table for a program

☐ Describe and identify syntax, execution and logic errors within a program

☐ Test that SQL statements work correctly

☐ Test that a website's links and navigation work as expected

☐ Test that all media files play or display as expected within web pages

☐ Test that web pages across a site are consistent

☐ Test that web pages match the wireframe user interface design

Evaluation

☐ Evaluate a program's fitness for purpose

☐ Evaluate how efficiently coding constructs have been used within a program

☐ Evaluate the robustness of a program

☐ Evaluate how readable a program is

☐ Evaluate a database solution or SQL statement in terms of fitness for purpose

☐ Evaluate a database solution or SQL statement in terms of accuracy of output

☐ Evaluate the fitness for purpose of a website solution

Key word glossary

Absolute addressing (p. 125)   a hyperlink shows the target location using the full URL or file location

Accuracy of output (p. 115)   how well do the results produced match what results you expected

Address bus (p. 97)   carries the address of a memory location from the processor to main memory, one direction only

Algorithm (p. 4)   a list of steps to solve a problem

Analysis stage (p. 2)   the developers look at the problem, discuss with the client and decide exactly what must be in the solution; the software specification is created

Anchor (p. 131)   when an element within a web page is assigned an id, then a hyperlink is created to jump straight to that element when the hyperlink is clicked

Arithmetic and logic unit (ALU) (p. 97)   performs all calculations and evaluates logical decisions; located within the processor

ASCII (p. 92)   see extended ASCII

Attribute (database) (p. 104)   a field attached to an entity

Attribute (vector graphics) (p. 92)   a characteristic of the object being drawn, e.g. line colour

Binary (p. 89)   the number system used by computers, made up of 0s and 1s

Bit (p. 90)   one binary digit, a 0 or a 1

Bit-mapped graphics (p. 94)   store graphics as a binary colour code for each pixel in the image

Boolean (p. 5)   true or false only

Browser (p. 125)   a program used to view web pages

Byte (p. 95)   eight bits

Cascading style sheets (CSS) (p. 132)   used to describe the layout and formatting of a web page

Central processing unit (CPU) (pp. 86, 96)   see processor

Character (p. 5)   any one punctuation symbol, letter or number that can be typed from the keyboard

Character set (p. 92)   the range of characters that can be represented

Colour depth (p. 94)   the number of bits used to store the colour code for each pixel in bit-mapped graphics; determines the number of available colours and the file size

Compiler (p. 99)   changes high-level program code into machine code, all at once; it saves the machine code version of the program

Compression (p. 123)   changes how data in a file is stored to take up less storage space

Condition (p. 76)   a logical statement that can be worked out to be true or false, e.g. age>13; uses logical operators such as =, >, <, <>, AND, OR

Conditional loop (p. 76)   DO … UNTIL …; repeatedly follows a group of instructions until a condition is met

Conditional statement (p. 74)   IF … THEN … ELSE … END IF; checks a condition once

Consistency (p. 136)   how well does the visual layout match across all the pages on a website

Construct (p. 10)   a common basic statement or group of statements of program code, such as a fixed loop, conditional loop or conditional statement

Control unit (p. 97)   decodes and executes instructions, keeps all components synchronised; located within the processor

Copyright, Designs and Patents Act 1988 (p. 121)   permission must be obtained from the creator of any material to legally use it (replaced by General Data Protection Regulation from 2018–19)

Data bus (p. 97)   carries data between the processor and main memory, either direction

Data dictionary (p. 103)   notation used to plan the structure of entities/tables with their attributes/fields and relationships within a database

Data Protection Act 1998 (p. 106)   the law that governs personal data; data must be held only with permission, only for the stated purposes and kept accurate and safe (replaced by General Data Protection Regulation from 2018–19)

Data structure (p. 4)   used to store data within a program, this can be either a variable or a one-dimensional (1D) array

Data type (p. 4)   the kind of data that can be stored within a data structure; one of character, string, integer, real or Boolean

Denary (p. 89)   a number system used by humans, with ten digits from 0 to 9

Design notation (p. 5)   the way developers write down their design

Design stage (p. 4)   the solution to the problem is planned, both the structure and the user interface

Development methodology (p. 1)   the approach that programmers take to solving the problem

Documentation stage (p. 85)   information to be distributed along with the program is created, usually including a user guide and technical guide

Dot notation (p. 112)   used when specifying entities and their attributes. In databases you would have <table name>.<field name>, for example Team.[Team ID]

Dots per inch (dpi) (p. 94)   the number of pixels along the line of one inch of an image

Efficient code (use of coding constructs) (p. 86)   whether the program code created contains unnecessary lines of code or repetition of code

Encryption (p. 101)   scrambling data into a code so that it cannot be understood if intercepted

End-user requirements (p. 103)   features that have to be included to ensure that users are able to access and carry out the functions of the database/website/program

Entity (database) (p. 104)   a table within a database

Entity-relationship diagram (p. 104)   a graphical design notation used to plan the relationships and structure of a database

Equi-join (p. 112)   used to represent a relationship between tables within an SQL query

Evaluation stage (p. 85)   developers look at their solution and decide how well it solves the original problem and how efficient the code is

Exceptional test data (p. 83)   data that should not be accepted, invalid entries

Execution error (p. 84)   an error that occurs while the program is running

Extended ASCII (p. 92)   an 8-bit code used to store characters

External hyperlink (p. 117)   a hyperlink that points to a page or file on a website which is different to the one that the link appears on

External stylesheet (p. 132)   a set of CSS rules contained within a separate file from any web pages that use them

Extreme test data (p. 83)   data on the edge of the acceptable range

Field length (p. 105)   the data entered into the field must meet certain requirements on the number of characters

Firewall (p. 100)   filters incoming (and outgoing) data packets to the network/system, which can prevent hackers from gaining access

Fitness for purpose (p. 86)   how well the solution solves the original problem

Fixed loop (p. 78)   FOR ... DO ... NEXT ...; repeatedly follows a group of instructions a set number of times

Floating point representation (pp. 55, 91) how computers store real numbers using mantissa and exponent

Flowchart (p. 5) a graphical design notation used to plan the structure of a program or system

Foreign key (p. 104) a field/attribute that appears in one table/entity but is the primary key of another table/entity; indicates a relationship

Form (database) (p. 106) a way of accepting input into a database system from users

Function (coding) (p. 5) a section of code that returns a value to the program

Functional requirements (p. 103) features that have to be included in order to solve the original problem given

General Data Protection Regulation (p. 107) data protection laws passed in 2018

Gibibyte (GiB) (p. 95) 1024 mebibytes

Hacking (p. 100) gaining access to data without permission

High-level language (p. 98) a programming language similar to English

Home page (p. 116) the first page that will be displayed in the browser when a user accesses a root URL

HTML (pp. 93, 125) Hypertext Markup Language; the language used to describe the content of web pages

Implementation stage (p. 2) the solution to the problem is created, whether a program, database or website

Indexing an array (p. 80) using a variable or value within brackets after the array name, to select only that element from the array

Input validation (p. 81) data entered is continually checked to ensure that it is valid

Integer (p. 5) a numeric data type, for whole numbers

Internal commentary (p. 88) lines within the program code that provide information for programmers; often called comments or remarks

Internal hyperlink (p. 117) a hyperlink that points to a page or file on the same website as the page that the link appears on

Internal stylesheet (p. 132) a set of CSS rules contained in the head section of a web page

Interpreter (p. 99) changes high-level program code into machine code, line by line; it does not save the machine code version of the program

Iterative (p. 2) a process that is repeated. In the software development process earlier stages are revisited as a result of information gained at later stages

JavaScript (p. 133) used to run program code within the browser on the user's computer

Kibibyte (KiB) (p. 95) 1024 bytes

Logic error (p. 84) an error that causes the program to produce incorrect results

Lossless compression (p. 123) reduces file size without losing any quality

Lossy compression (p. 123) loses some quality to produce a smaller file size

Low-fidelity prototype (p. 122) a drawing on paper of a web page or screen; often used to test the user interface with prospective users before creating the website or product

Machine code (p. 98) the language made up of 1s and 0s that computers require programs to be translated into

Main memory (p. 97) the area where open programs and the associated data are stored while they are running

Mebibyte (MiB) (p. 95) 1024 kibibytes

Memory location (p. 97) a unique area of memory within the main memory

Normal test data (p. 83) data well within the acceptable range

One-dimensional array (p. 4) holds a number of items of data, all of the same data type

Onmouseout (p.134) JavaScript mouse event that runs a subprogram when the pointer moves off of the specified element of the web page

Onmouseover (p. 134) a JavaScript mouse event that runs a subprogram when the pointer hovers over the specified element of the web page

Ordered list (p. 127) a list produced using HTML where each item in the list is numbered

Parameter (p. 81) a piece of data sent into a function that the function needs to do its job

Pixel (p. 93) one small square that, when combined with others, makes up an image on screen or is saved as part of a bit-mapped graphic

Predefined function (p. 81) a section of code that returns a value to the program that was created by the creators of the programming language

Presence check (p. 105) a field must have data entered for every record

Primary key (p. 104) a field/attribute that will have unique contents within a table/entity and so can be used to uniquely identify each record the table/entity contains

Processor (p. 96)   the part of the computer that works out what the program's instructions mean and ensures they are carried out

Pseudocode (p. 5)   a textual design notation used to plan the structure of a program

Query (p. 106)   a search and/or sort performed to obtain selected records from the database

Random access memory (RAM) (p. 97)   used for main memory, this kind of memory requires power to store data and its contents can be changed

Range (database validation) (p. 105)   the data entered into the field must be within certain limits

Readability (coding) (p. 83)   how easy the code is to read and understand

Readability (user interface) (p. 120)   how easily the information on a page/screen can be understood by the user

Read only memory (ROM) (p. 97)   system memory which holds vital systems information, for example, start-up instructions

Real (p. 5)   a numeric data type, for numbers with a fractional part, e.g. 3.75

Referential integrity (p. 109)   data entered into a foreign key must equal an item of data held in the primary key of the related table

Register (p. 97)   a small fast area of temporary memory storage within the processor

Relative addressing (p. 125)   a hyperlink showing the target location using the current page location as a starting point within the folders on the website

Resolution (p. 94)   the number of pixels that make up an image

Resolution independence (p. 95)   vector graphics can be scaled up with no loss of quality

Restricted choice (p. 105)   the data entered into the field must be selected from a list of valid possibilities

Robustness (p. 87)   how well the system avoids crashing when invalid data is entered

Sampling rate (p. 124)   the number of times in one second that a measurement of a sound wave has been taken and saved

Software specification (p. 3)   a clear statement of the problem to be solved including functional requirements, user requirements, inputs and outputs

SQL (p. 111)   structured query language; the language used to interact with databases

Standard algorithm (p. 79)   a list of steps agreed as the best way to solve a common programming problem

Standard file format (p. 118)   a way of saving data that can be opened and used on many different programs and systems

String (p. 5)   a sequence of characters

Structure diagram (p. 5)   a graphical design notation used to plan the structure of a program

Syntax error (p. 84)   an error resulting from breaking the rules of the language

Tebibyte (TiB) (p. 95)   1024 gibibytes

Technical guide (p. 85)   explains how to install the program and states the system requirements

Testing stage (p. 83)   the solution is tested using a test plan to ensure that it solves the original problem

Transparency (p. 116)   part of the graphic can be fully or partially see-through allowing underlying graphics to be seen

Traversing (p. 79)   moving across; in N5 this usually means looping to check the contents of an array

Unordered list (p. 127)   a list produced using HTML where each item in the list is preceded by a bullet point

URL (p. 101)   uniform resource locator; a web address

User guide (p. 85)   explains how to operate the program

Valid (p. 3)   sensible data that satisfies the limits of input validation and should be accepted as input; normal and extreme test data will be valid

Validation (database) (p. 105)   rules are applied to the data entered into a field/attribute

Variable (p. 34)   holds one item of data that can change when the program is run

Vector graphic (p. 93)   stores a graphic as text, listing objects and their attributes

Visual layout (p. 119)   how the information on a screen is presented

Wireframe (p. 120)   a graphical design notation used to plan the user interface of a program, web page, or database form/report

Answers

Chapter 1 Analysis and design (software), p.1.

1 I have to write a program that will tell users whether or not they will have speed bumps installed within their housing estate.
The program must accept and validate a number of homes more than zero, loop for that number of homes, accept and validate the residents' votes of 'yes' or 'no', show the total number of 'yes' votes on the screen, check if the number of 'yes' votes is greater than half the number of homes and show a relevant message on the screen.

Inputs
- Homes: an integer number variable that must be validated to be greater than zero.
- Vote: a string variable that must be validated to be 'yes' or 'no'.

Process
- Total up the votes, divide homes by 2, check number of 'yes' votes against this.

Outputs
- The total number of 'yes' votes, a message indicating if the estate will have speed bumps installed or not.

2 A development methodology is the approach that the programmers take to solve the problem.

3 a) An iterative process is a process that repeats.
   b) The software development process is an iterative process because earlier stages in the process often have to be revisited as a result of information gained at later stages in the process.

4 The software specification is a clear statement of the problem to be solved.

5 When an array is declared you must state the name you're giving to the array, the data type of the data that it will store, and the number of elements in the array.

6 a) A number containing a decimal point such as 5.7.
   b) Only 'true' or 'false'.

7 The way that the programmer writes down their plan to solve the problem.

Answers

Chapter 4 Implementation (reading and interpreting code) p.72

1 Line 1 declares a real variable called price and sets its contents to 12.99.
Line 2 gets input from the keyboard and puts in the integer variable called 'order'.
Line 3 multiplies the price by the order and puts the answer into the variable called 'total'.
Line 4 shows the contents of the total variable on the screen.

2 Line 1 declares a character variable called 'initial'.
Line 2 shows a message on the screen to ask the user for input.
Line 3 gets input from the keyboard and puts in the character variable called 'initial'.

3 Line 1 gets input from the keyboard and puts in the integer variable called 'player_rating'.
Line 2 starts a conditional statement, if the content of the player_rating variable is less than 65.
Line 3 the string variable category is assigned the content 'Bronze'.
Line 4 otherwise if the content of the player_rating variable is less than 75.
Line 5 the string variable category is assigned the content 'Silver'.
Line 6 otherwise.
Line 7 the string variable category is assigned the content 'Gold'.

4 Line 8 should be END IF.

5 Line 1 starts a conditional loop.
Line 2 shows a message on the screen to ask the user to answer a question.
Line 3 gets input from the keyboard and puts in the variable called 'number'.
Line 4 ends the conditional loop when the content of the number variable is 8.

6 Line 1 gets input from the keyboard and puts in the real variable called 'multiple'.
Line 2 starts a fixed loop for ten times.
Line 3 multiplies the times variable by the multiple variable and puts the answer into the variable called 'answer'.
Line 4 shows a message on the screen that includes the content of the multiple variable, the times variable and the answer variable.
Line 5 ends the fixed loop.

7 $2 \times 1 = 2$
$2 \times 2 = 4$
$2 \times 3 = 6$
$2 \times 4 = 8$
$2 \times 5 = 10$
$2 \times 6 = 12$
$2 \times 7 = 14$
$2 \times 8 = 16$
$2 \times 9 = 18$
$2 \times 10 = 20$

Answers

Chapter 5 Testing, documentation and evaluation (software) p.83

1 They can look back at their analysis to ensure all parts of the problem are tested. They can use a range of normal, extreme and exceptional data.

2 Normal: any real number from 0.02 to 349.99
   Extreme: 0.01 or 350
   Exceptional: 0 or a negative number or a number more than 350 or text

3 A syntax error (`PRINT` has been misspelled).

4 a) An execution error, as it crashed while running.
   b) Exceptional test data, as 7 is higher than the acceptable range.
   c) Input validation.

5 The analysis stage and the testing stage.

6 An execution error.

7 So that other people can understand the code and maintain it if necessary.

Answers

Chapter 6 Data representation p.89

1 A whole number.

2 $1 + 2 + 4 + 32 + 64 = 103$

3 10111000 ($128 + 32 + 16 + 8 = 184$)

4 The mantissa is 10101, the exponent is -111.

5 A character that doesn't show on the screen.

6 The range of the characters available to the user.

7 'Hello' has five letters. Each letter takes up 8 bits. $5 \times 8 = 40$ bits (which is 5 bytes).

8 There are 256 possible characters in the extended ASCII character set ($2^8 = 256$).

9 Vector

10 Bitmap

11 Vector

12 Bitmap

Answers

Chapter 7 Computer structure p.96

1 a) The data bus.
   b) In a register.
2 It performs all calculations and makes all the decisions.
3 Each has a unique address.
4 Binary numbers: 1s and 0s.
5 Interpreter
6 Compiler

Answers

Chapter 8 Security and the environment p.100

1 Use a firewall; encrypt your data before sending or storing.
2 The data will all be in a code; it will look like nonsense.
3 Burning of fossil fuels causes air pollution and increases global warming.
4 It turns off the monitor, the hard drive and possibly the processor.

Answers

Chapter 9 Analysis and design (database) p.103

1 Data to be stored and queries to be performed.
2 a) The name of the primary key will be underlined, inside an oval joined to the entity name by a line.
   b) The name of the foreign key will end with an asterisk (*), inside an oval joined to the entity name by a line.
3 The foreign key is always an attribute of the entity on the 'many' side of the relationship.
4 Boolean
5 The data entered into the field must be selected from a list of valid possibilities.
6 Range validation/check
7 Force the user to enter data in the field.

Answers

Chapter 10 Implementation (database) p.108

1
```
SELECT * FROM Charity;
```

2 Shows all the fields from the Charity table but only those records where the charity focuses on Homelessness.

3
```
SELECT Name, Focus FROM Charity;
```

4
```
SELECT * FROM Charity ORDER BY Name ASC;
```

5 Removes all records from the Charity table.

6
```
DELETE FROM Charity WHERE Focus="Animals";
```

Answers

Chapter 12 Analysis and design (web) p.116

1 An internal hyperlink points to a page or file on the same site. An external hyperlink points to a page or file on another website.
2 The page or file that your hyperlink points to may be changed, moved or removed as you have no control over the external website.
3 No, he has not broken the Copyright, Designs and Patents Act (1988) because he has the creator's permission.
4 So that users are more likely to be able to open the files, as standard file formats can be opened by a wide range of different programs.
5 Lower file size will save backing storage space, and lower file size will improve download times.
6 GIF and PNG
7 GIF supports animation; PNG has more colours/a higher colour depth (bit depth).
8 The file size would get smaller.
9 The file size would increase.

Answers

Chapter 13 Implementation (web) p.125

1 `</HTML>`

2 `<TITLE>` and `<LINK>`

3 Six, from `<H1>` to `<H6>`

4 **1** Alan
- Carrie
- Alynna

   2 Bob

5 Relative addressing states the file's location using the location of the current page as a starting point. Absolute addressing states the file's location using the full URL or file path.

6 `<IMG>`

7 The browser will show audio controls such as play, pause and volume which the user can interact with.

8 An id must be unique; an element can have only one id; no two elements may have the same id. A class is not unique; an element may have multiple classes, and multiple elements may have the same class.

9 The '#' character.

10 The external stylesheet can be downloaded once and applied to multiple pages, improving access times. The external stylesheet will ensure consistency across multiple pages, which is user-friendly.

11
```
<LINK rel="stylesheet" type="text/css"
href="superstyle.css">
```

12
```
H2 { font-size:18px;}
```

13 All elements with the class 'description' will be centred and set to Calibri font or similar. The external stylesheet can be created and applied to multiple pages, improving development time.

14
```
#special { background-color:green;} or
   #special { background-color:#00ff00;}
```

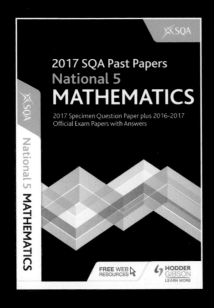
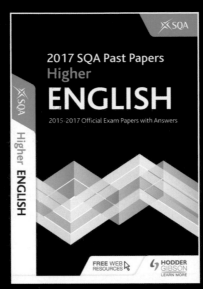